motorcycling
abroad

ADVENTURE • ADVICE • SAFETY • LAWS

© Peter Henshaw, 2006

First published February 2006

Every effort has been made to ensure the accuracy of the
information given but the author and the publisher accept no
responsibility for any injury, loss or inconvenience sustained by
anyone using this guide. If you have any comments, information
or photographs which would be useful to include in future editions
of *Motorcycling Abroad*, please send them to Books Division,
Haynes Publishing, Sparkford, Yeovil, Somerset BA22 7JJ.

ISBN 1 84425 245 0

British Library Cataloguing in Publication Data
A catalogue record for this book is available from the British Library

Printed by J. H. Haynes & Co. Ltd, Sparkford, Yeovil, Somerset BA22 7JJ, UK

Haynes Publishing
Sparkford, Yeovil, Somerset BA22 7JJ
Telephone: **01963 442030**
Fax: **01963 440001**
E-mail: **sales@haynes.co.uk**
Web site: **www.haynes.co.uk**

motorcycling
abroad

ADVENTURE • ADVICE • SAFETY • LAWS

PETER HENSHAW

CONTENTS

Riding in Southern Europe

152

Riding in Eastern Europe

170

Riding in North America

184

Riding in Australasia

194

Riding further afield

204

MOTORCYCLING
ABROAD

Riding a motorcycle abroad is a joyful, liberating experience, something that everyone with a bike licence should do at least once. There's nothing to compare with rolling off the ferry on a well-laden bike, and heading for the horizon. Beyond the confines of the British Isles (beautiful though they are) there's a huge selection of roads, cultures and scenery just waiting to be explored: mountains, valleys, plains and lakes, magical coastlines and tranquil rolling hills, all just a ferry-ride away.

7

Better still, all of this is easier to access than ever before. The advent of the Euro, and the near universal acceptance of credit cards, is making long distance motorcycle touring easier too. More and more UK motorcyclists are heading overseas every year. If you want more of a challenge – maybe riding to North Africa, or around South-East Asia or New Zealand – this is possible as well. If you don't want to ride on your own, there are plenty of companies offering organised tours: they take care of the route and accommodation and can even provide a bike, so all you need to do is turn up and enjoy the ride.

That's not so say that there aren't plenty of hazards on the way, and this book aims to make you aware of them, as well as offering advice on how to prepare for the big trip. You still need to have a measure of self-reliance, but that's part of the attraction of motorcycle touring – even a long weekend in northern France can be a mini-adventure. Open to the weather, the scenery and life in general, riding a motorcycle abroad can deliver a wonderful holiday.

Dry roads, good weather and the freedom of two wheels – there are few better ways to spend your holidays

Many countries abroad, especially in Europe, positively welcome motorcyclists, as this sign in Austria demonstrates

Guided or solo?

Once you've decided to take the plunge and ride your bike abroad, the next question is do you do it on your own, or take advantage of a guided tour? Ten years ago the question would hardly have been relevant, but today guided motorcycle tours are on offer to just about everywhere in the world, whether you're interested in a weekend in France, two weeks in the Czech Republic, or a more adventurous trip north to the Arctic Circle or south into the Sahara. Even if you want to try biking somewhere really exotic, flying out to Thailand or India and hiring a bike when you get there, there are companies that will organise all of this for you, at a price.

That's the chief attraction of guided tours – they should take all the hassle out of long-distance biking. It's really the two-wheel equivalent of a package tour, with hotels and ferries pre-booked, routes worked out and an English-speaking guide always on hand. Exactly what's included varies from tour to tour, so make sure you are clear about this before booking. Some tour leaders require that you ride in groups, others let everyone go at their own pace, meeting up at a hotel each evening. But whatever the exact format, guided tours take a lot of the worry out of biking abroad, especially for novices. Actually, many experienced bikers prefer to tour this way – they're not nervous about riding abroad, but just like the hassle-free aspect.

Another variation is fly/ride, popular in the US. Here the company provides a bike, an itinerary, and can book accommodation, but you ride on your own. Guided tours and fly/rides aren't cheap, though. In 2005, four days in Spain cost around £400 (including a guide, accommodation and some meals) while a two-week guided ride around New Zealand, including guide, bike hire and accommodation, was around £2,750.

Of course, making your own arrangements is far cheaper, and has advantages of its own. Apart from ferry timetables, you're completely free to ride

MOTORCYCLING **ABROAD**

wherever and whenever you want, or to indulge in a couple of days of sightseeing off the bike. Local tourist information centres will be happy to help you book accommodation (it is, after all, what they're there for), though it may be worthwhile booking ahead in more remote areas or at the height of the season, rather than relying on pot luck. Touring solo means relying on your own resources to deal with such minor or major problems that may arise. But for some, that mini-adventure is part of what motorcycling abroad is all about.

Women and motorcycle touring

Birgit Schunemann has ridden her BMW through Africa, Asia, Europe and the Americas. Here's her advice to women bikers:

"You ride a motorcycle? What happens if you drop it? Are you able to pick it up?" Sooner or later, every female motorcyclist gets asked this question – a lot of blokes aren't able to pick up their own bikes, but funnily enough they hardly ever get asked. The truth is that riding a bike abroad is no more difficult for a woman than a man, just different.

Whether you want to ride pillion or on your own bike is down to personal preference. I like to do both, as each has its advantages – as pillion, you don't have the kudos of riding, but you do get a chance to look around. In any case, you are never 'just' a pillion: rider and pillion are a team, and the trip will only succeed if both play their part in planning, navigation and loading the bike.

When riding solo I prefer to ride my own bike, an old BMW R60/5 named Henry. I take care of maintenance and repairs too – that way I know what's been done, and the experience means that I'm able to help myself out on the road. The frustrating thing is that mechanics still assume they need to talk to my partner Sam, though they soon pick up the point that I'm the person they need to speak to. Once they've taken that on board, they're very helpful.

Set the pace
When in a group, ride at the pace of the slowest bike, or arrange to meet up later. A group atmosphere can be soured stupidly by an imbalance in ability, and too many deaths are caused by speed under pressure. The point is to have a good time.

10

Many women have ridden their own bikes around Europe and all over the world, and in some cases they may find travel easier. The moral seems to be – go for it!

One day in Guatemala I was working on my bike in the courtyard of the hospedaje we were staying in, while Sam was doing our laundry. The lady running the hostel was aghast: "In Guatemala we do things the right way," she said. "The man repairs the car and we women do the washing." Mind you, that evening she offered to swap her husband for my other half when she saw him cooking the dinner!

The best preparation you can do before a big trip is to gain confidence in riding your bike fully laden. Load up carefully for good weight distribution, then find an empty supermarket car park and practice U-turns and low-speed slaloms – it'll pay dividends later on. I went on a beginners' off-road course, which is worth doing even if you're never planning to ride on the dirt: it teaches you so much about bike control and general confidence.

Don't take too many clothes. For riding through Africa, South, Central and North America I took my bike gear, two T-shirts, three pairs of knickers, three pairs of socks, a pair of jeans, a long-sleeved shirt, a fleece, and flip-flops. In Africa I added a long skirt and a sarong. Take a look at colours, because a tad of mixing and matching can change really casual kit into gear for a good night out. This collection is enough even when it's cold – you can layer your clothes to the level of warmth you need.

When off the bike I try to blend in to the local

customs as far as possible – for one thing this makes you less vulnerable. I was given far more respect when I covered up in countries where you don't find local women wearing shorts or mini skirts, and managed to get far better prices in the markets too. But the right clothing doesn't always protect you from unwanted male attention, so don't take any abuse if you've done everything you can to respect local customs. I was groped once, but a good left hook quickly put the bloke off – he legged it! And tampons? The simple rule (if you're riding through remote areas) is to stock up in major cities.

I really enjoy connecting with other women, especially in less well-off countries. Even if language isn't shared, smiles say a lot; doors will be opened to you as a woman that will never be opened to a man. The downside is accepting that some cultures are demeaning towards women, though I did manage to turn that to my advantage once. Working at getting our bikes out of Mombasa, I was endlessly hassled by a customs official after baksheesh. In the end, I told him that I wasn't allowed to make decisions regarding money and would have to ask my man. He never bothered me again.

Being a woman and touring by motorcycle are two worlds that fit together well. Lots of women do it, so go for it!

Meeting point
Another group riding tip. If everyone wants to ride at different speeds, it might make more sense to have a clear meeting point and time later in the day. That way, everyone can ride at their own pace. It's a good idea to have an emergency meeting point anyway, in case the group gets split up.

11

Travelling in a group brings its own rewards. Some riders prefer the ultimate freedom of going solo, but being part of a group is a good idea for first-time travellers

ON THE ROAD

Riding abroad for the first time can seem like learning to ride all over again. Even actions that are second nature at home – like filling up with fuel or whipping through a roundabout – can be confusing and challenging in unfamiliar surroundings.

But just as you gradually gained confidence after learning to ride for the first time, exactly the same thing happens as the kilometres mount overseas. Even after just a couple of days you may wonder why you were ever nervous in the first place. But however confident and experienced you are, you still need that extra level of vigilance when riding abroad. Headlight flashes, for example, mean different things in different countries. Being prepared (which includes having the right bike for the trip you're intending to make) will make it easier to adjust.

It looks idyllic, and it is, but being out on the road abroad does call for extra vigilance, especially if you've never done it before. This is the Picos de Europa, northern Spain

A touring bike like this BMW K1200RS, with a screen, fairing and fitted luggage, will eat up the miles effortlessly, but really you can tour on anything

Choosing a bike

A lot of people assume that to ride abroad, or do any long distance touring, you need a large, expensive well-equipped tourer. Well, you don't – but the type of bike you choose will determine the sort of trip you can comfortably manage.

It's horses for courses. If you want to get across Europe in a few days (albeit long, high-mileage days) – if you want to bike down to the south of France, or Italy, or into Eastern Europe as quickly as possible, for instance – then there are few better ways to do it than on something like a Honda Pan European or BMW RT or LT. Try it on a much smaller bike with no fairing, and you'll be terminally tired by the end of the first day.

Big tourers make 500-mile days not only possible but comfortable; smaller bikes don't, unless you're impervious to discomfort. Modern tourers offer luxury features that would have seemed outlandish not so long ago: heated handlebar grips and seats to cope with chilly mornings; on-bike sound systems and rider/pillion intercoms to while away the long autoroute miles; anti-lock brakes, electric screens and efficient, aerodynamic fairings. They often come with capacious, weatherproof factory-fitted luggage as well, and have the sort of effortless performance that takes the slog out of riding long distances at speed. And there's no chain to worry about – all serious tourers have maintenance-free shaft drive.

All this comes at a price though. A new, fully-equipped Pan Euro or BMW will cost over £10,000 to put on the road, and will also be expensive to run and insure. Unless the bike is your primary form of transport all year round, this makes for an expensive hobby. Expensive bikes are also more attractive to thieves, wherever you are.

However, to term such bikes as 'tourers' is something of a misnomer, as all motorcycles – and even scooters – are capable of touring. The key thing is to be realistic about what your bike can manage, in a way that you are happy with. A friend of mine rode down to the Sahara on a Yamaha Townmate, a diminutive 80cc scooter. Equipped with spare tyres and fuel cans, he pottered down through France, Spain and Morocco at 40-50mph. He made it to the desert as well, and if the scooter got stuck in Saharan sand, then he hopped off and walked alongside until it was free. Of course, not everyone has the time or patience to go touring on a step-through, but the point is that you can if you have the inclination. The same goes for small motorcycles, such as 500cc road bikes and 250cc traillies. Nick Sanders, who for some time held the Guinness Record as fastest man around the world on a 150mph Triumph Daytona 900, did his first round-the-world trip on a Royal Enfield Bullet 350, the two-wheeled equivalent of the Morris Minor.

Bikes like these do have their limitations. You can't expect to cover as many miles in a day as on a big machine, or carry as much luggage, though the 400-650cc big scooters (known as super-scooters) offer good weather protection, decent motorway performance and even some luggage room.

If you want to take on a more challenging ride, such as off-road across Africa, then 500 or 650cc is more sensible, giving the power needed to plough through soft sand and rutted roads. Overlanders – the serious long-distance bike travellers – tend to favour a minimum of 500cc and dual-purpose machines that are as at home on sandy or gravel tracks as they are on tarmac. Dual-purpose tyres ('knobblies'), long-travel suspension and plenty of ground clearance are the key features of one of these, along with a comfortable, upright riding position.

BMW once had a near monopoly on purpose-built touring bikes, offering reliability, shaft drive and a long range. There's a lot more choice now though

Sometimes termed 'adventure tourers', these bikes are strong and adaptable, and able to carry a great deal of luggage plus rider and pillion. The BMW GS series (as used by actors Ewan McGregor and Charlie Boorman on their round-the-world trip in 2004) is a favourite of overlanders, as are the Honda Africa Twin and Yamaha Tenere. If you're not heading off-road, one of the new generation of softer adventure tourers, like the Triumph Tiger or Honda Varadero, could fit the bill. These are more road-oriented than the genuine dual-purpose machines, heavier, but more comfortable. If you're planning on a good proportion of off-road going, then one of the lighter single-cylinder bikes from any of the Japanese manufacturers, KTM of Austria or BMW's F650GS would be a better bet.

At the other end of the biking scale are cruisers. There's a tendency in motorcycling to dismiss Harley-Davidsons and similar machines as suitable only for Sunday afternoon jaunts, but they can make surprisingly capable tourers. Over a long distance the laidback riding position isn't actually as comfortable as it looks, but keep the speed down (and/or fit a screen) and they can work well. They're big enough to carry a lot of weight, and most cruisers have maintenance-free final drives – either a shaft or a toothed belt.

Bouncing off to another extreme, one might think that sports bikes are totally unsuitable for touring abroad, but some riders do use them. In the summer, one can see groups of R1s and GSX-Rs heading over to big race meetings in France, Germany or Holland, or maybe to play in the mountain passes of the Alps or the Pyrenees. There's now a choice of suitable sports bike luggage, though other factors still limit their usefulness for long-distance riding: tyre life (as little as 3,000 miles on the rear); tank range; and an uncomfortable riding position at low speeds. Sports bikes are also bad news for pillions over distance, so choosing one of these for two-up touring may be down to a lack of pillion power! A sports tourer, such as the benchmark Honda VFR or Triumph Sprint ST, is a good compromise. These bikes are almost as fast and

ON THE ROAD

slick-handling as the true sports bikes, but can take hard luggage (see below) and are kinder to pillions.

Whatever bike you choose to ride abroad, there are a few fundamentals to bear in mind. How big is the fuel tank and how far will it take you? What sort of luggage will fit, and how easily? What sort of mileage will the bike comfortably manage in a day? And of course, will it be fun to ride? As long as it's suitable for your planned trip and the way you ride, any bike can take you touring beyond Britain.

Preparing the bike

It sounds obvious, but your bike needs to be prepared for its trip abroad. However reliable it may be on a 20-mile-a-day commute, conditions will be tougher on holiday. You'll be covering more miles each day; the bike will be laden with luggage and/or a pillion; and there may be a lot of hot motorway miles to contend with. And if the worst does happen you'll either have to communicate the trouble to a dealer, handle it yourself or have the bike trailered home on the recovery insurance.

On the premise that prevention of any of this is better than cure, the bike needs to be fully serviced before departure: engine/transmission oil changed, plus all the filters, and a thorough check over. Even if you think you'll be back home before the next service is due, it's still worth erring on the side of caution. Take the chain and sprockets, or the brake pads – are they up to a 2,000-mile ride across Europe? If in doubt, ask the dealer. Better to spend a little extra now than to regret it on a lonely Spanish roadside. Whoever carries out the service may notice frayed wiring, or a cable on its last legs, which otherwise might fail a few days into the trip. Of course, all these things can be repaired abroad (even if you're heading somewhere quite remote), but it's just less hassle to sort them out before you go.

The same goes for tyres. Modern, heavy, high performance motorcycles do get through tyres, and riding a heavily-laden machine fast along hot tarmac

Get covered
Splash out on breakdown and recovery insurance (see page 80). It'll bring peace of mind, and if the worst does happen, will save you a fortune in both time and money.

17

Adventure tourers are an increasingly popular for doing distance. They're roomy, comfortable and have plenty of luggage potential, but don't take the off-road looks too seriously

is the quickest way to wear rubber out. This is especially true of sports bikes like the Yamaha R1 or Honda FireBlade, plus the hyper-fast Suzuki Hyabusa and Kawasaki ZX-12R – ridden hard, these can need a new rear tyre in 3,000 miles or less.

So check that your tyres will comfortably last the entire trip, before reaching the UK legal minimum of at least 1mm of tread for a continuous band over at least three-quarters of the width of the tyre. Correct inflation (bearing in mind the extra weight of a passenger and/or luggage) is also essential. If you're likely to need fresh rubber out on the road, you should be able to check with the manufacturer regarding the availability of the correct type and speed-rated tyre in the area you're heading for. Thanks to the wonders of e-mail, you may even be able to check direct with a local dealer.

All of this applies to road bikes, but things are slightly different for those heading into Africa on a traillie. Ideally, one needs serious knobbly tyres for the sandy pistes, but these have inferior handling to road tyres on tarmac, and wear out more quickly. Many travellers strap the knobblies on as luggage, and swap tyres when they reach the desert. But for tarmac-only road trips through Europe or America, things are far more simple. Modern tyres (especially the tubeless type) might be more tricky to change, but they rarely puncture. Look after your tyres, to paraphrase an old saying, and they'll look after you.

Another important point to consider before heading off is suspension adjustment. It's important because (unless you're in the credit-card-and-toothbrush school of travelling light) the bike will be carrying more weight than usual, especially if two-up. Most motorcycles have some sort of suspension adjustment, but we're not concerned with the multi-adjustable front forks of sports bikes. All you need to do is turn up the pre-load on the rear spring, to enable it to cope with the higher load; the damping may be adjustable as well. The owner's handbook should tell you how to do all of this. Failure to stiffen up the rear suspension will result in soggy, wallowy handling and more strain on the rear suspension and tyre.

So, we have a bike in excellent standard condition, freshly serviced and with new tyres. Does it need modifying? This really depends on where you're going. Adventurous types heading overland to India or South Africa can choose from a whole range of changes that will render their bike better able to cope with tough conditions. Bash plates prevent sharp rocks puncturing the crankcase; extra-large fuel tanks can extend your range up to 500 miles or more; and in desert conditions, a hard-working air-cooled engine will benefit from an oil cooler.

For less ambitious touring there's less to do, but the nice thing is that many modifications will prove just as useful when you get home. A plate welded on to the sidestand, for example, works as well in a muddy English field as it does in an Austrian campsite. An automatic chain oiler, such as the Scottoiler, takes the everyday maintenance out of living with a chain, whether commuting or touring. It's also worth considering weather protection. A naked bike may be very pleasant on a short Sunday ride, but the charm can fade during a week of solid rain on holiday. Fitting a screen will make a big difference, especially on motorways, and there's a huge variety to choose from. Finally, take a spare ignition key, and keep it somewhere safe.

Vital spares only
Don't be tempted to take a huge selection of spares as some sort of comfort blanket. They'll weigh a ton and take up valuable luggage space. If your bike is in tip-top condition before you set off then you should hardly need a thing anyway. But if your bike has a weakness, then carry that part for peace of mind, especially if it's a rare one.

19

Overlanding on a budget? The owner of this elderly 250cc Honda XL trail bike was just setting off for South Africa

With heavy luggage and maybe a passenger on board, tyre pressures will need to be higher than normal – check the handbook

Maintenance and repairs

The best form of maintenance is of the preventative kind, so keep an eye on your bike during the trip. It's good to get into a morning routine of checking the oil level, the chain tension and for tyre damage, plus a general walk around to check that all is well on the bike. Even during the day, visually check any strapped-down luggage whenever you stop. Tyre pressures should be checked weekly.

Breaking down is a source of great concern to many riders. Unless you are super-confident about your own abilities, breakdown/recovery insurance (see page 80) is essential for peace of mind. But that really applies only to Europe and North America. For more adventurous trips across remote areas, you need to be more self-reliant. For anyone contemplating that kind of trip, being able to change tyres and repair punctures is an essential skill, as is curing electrical or fuel faults.

Finally, a word on tools and spares. Modern bikes rarely break down, so it really isn't worth taking a vast selection of hardware with you. Tools and spares are heavy, and take up valuable space, so it makes sense to take the minimum necessary. For Europe, a basic set of tools, spare clutch and throttle cables and a selection of fuses will be sufficient. Even if you can't fit these yourself, it could save time by preventing your having to wait for spares to be ordered locally. Zip ties have a thousand and one uses, and if you do get your hands dirty a sachet of hand cleaner will be worth its weight in gold.

Even when riding further afield, getting hold of spares should not be a problem. International couriers such as DHL can deliver to most areas of the globe within a few days, though it will speed things up if you have an efficient dealer back at home, who knows what you're doing and what you need. They can order the part for you, so if you're planning a long trip it's well worth cultivating a good dealer.

Befriend your dealer

Make a friend of your local dealer. When they know where you're going and all your bike details, they'll be able to send parts out to you much faster. Using an international courier such as TNT will be quicker than conventional post and will deal with the inevitable customs hassle. If you're leaving Europe, give the dealer a copy of your carnet, which will avoid import tax on the spare part.

Luggage

For car drivers, carrying luggage is easy – just chuck it all in the boot, and away you go. But motorcycle luggage takes more thinking about. Ideally, it should not only be tough, waterproof and secure, but also smart enough to carry into a hotel lobby without looking out of place. Some of it will meet all those criteria, at a price.

A few motorcycles come with built-in luggage as standard, but they can be counted on the fingers of one hand. The Honda Goldwing, BMW K1200LT and certain Harley-Davidsons are examples. Many others can have luggage fitted as a dealer option. All scooters, of course, come with some capacity, though even on the big superscooters this is normally limited to space for a helmet plus odds and ends.

For most of us, luggage has to be bought later on, as an extra, and there is a choice of two basic systems: hard or soft. Which one you go for will probably come down to how much you have to spend. Soft luggage is much cheaper, with a pair of panniers starting at around £90. These clip on to a harness in a couple of seconds, so they're very convenient to use. There's a huge range of shapes, sizes and colours on offer, and most are expandable, with extra pockets to take small items. Being soft, they're also unlikely to damage themselves or anything else if you misjudge that filtering manoeuvre. However, there are some downsides. While soft luggage can be clipped on very quickly, it can be unclipped just as easily, and by anyone who takes a fancy to it. Exposed zips are not secure, nor are they waterproof, so your luggage will need to be wrapped in plastic bags to keep it dry.

Most of the same comments apply to tankbags, though many of these can be unzipped and taken with you as a small rucksack, so security isn't such an issue. It's a good idea to keep all your valuables in the tankbag, and leave dirty laundry in the panniers. Not everyone likes tankbags, as they place weight high up and can be intrusive while you're riding. But

21

World of biking

I was getting complacent about the reliability of my Honda Transalp, which always started and never seemed to go wrong. Stopping for fuel one day, I was shocked to notice that A wheel-retaining cap had cracked right across, a potentially dangerous fault that grounded the bike until I could get a new part. Even modern bikes need regularly checking over.

Hard luggage is neater than the fabric variety, more secure and usually more waterproof into the bargain. It's more expensive though, and heavier too

This Yamaha TDM toured Iceland and the Faroes with Oxford soft panniers and tankbag. For day trips, we left the quickly detachable panniers wherever we were staying, and just used the tankbag

they are easy and convenient to use, and the magnetic type will plonk straight on to a steel fuel tank. The clip-on type take longer for the initial fitting, but once in place are just as convenient. Most tankbags have a clear map pocket on top (not to be used while riding) and all sorts of pockets and cubbyholes.

Hard luggage – a set of panniers and/or a topbox – is a more expensive option, with panniers starting at around £280 (plus mounting frames) and a complete set costing £700 or more. The good news is that hard luggage is (usually) waterproof, looks smart and is far more secure than the soft kind. It can be locked to the bike, but still unclipped fairly easily, if you have a key. Hard panniers can also be made more capacious than soft ones, so a couple should find plenty of room for a week away, and some topboxes are big enough to accept two full-face helmets. Finally, in the event of an accident hard luggage will do a better job of protecting the contents. If you can afford it, hard luggage has few disadvantages, though it is heavier, and large panniers will add considerably to the width of the bike.

Most hard luggage is made of plastic, though aluminium luggage is now becoming increasingly popular as well. The latter is favoured by serious overlanders, as aluminium panniers are more robust than conventional boxes, and if you do fall off they can usually be hammered back into shape: plastic panniers usually split on impact. Again, not a cheap option, at around £500 for a set of panniers and frames, but they do look the business.

If a complete set of panniers and topbox still doesn't give enough capacity, there's only one answer for motorcycling abroad – a trailer. This is the most expensive option of all, starting at around £1,000, plus the cost of fitting a tow bar to your bike. But for sheer capacity, they can't be beaten, and are ideal if you're taking camping gear as well. A well-designed bike-specific trailer will not interfere with the handling of the bike at all – in fact it makes less difference than a set of heavily-laden panniers and topbox. But there are certain restrictions to their size and weight in Europe, and it's worth checking on their legality elsewhere before you arrive.

One final word on luggage. Don't be tempted to carry everything in a large backpack. It may be a fraction of the price of proper bike luggage, but you'll have to carry it everywhere with you. A loaded backpack could also compromise your safety if you come off. Stick to the real thing.

Keep weight low down
Pack heavy items at the bottom of your luggage, which will keep the bike's centre of gravity low, making it easier to handle. Luggage should be within the bike's wheelbase as well. It also makes things easier when packing and unpacking if you can avoid hefting heavy items in and out every day.

Aluminium panniers are the ultimate luggage for serious overlanders. Not cheap, but much tougher than hard plastic panniers if the bike goes down. They also add an undeniable Sahara-ready chic

Well laden for the big trip – note the well travelled panniers, old army rucksacks as front bags, slung over the fuel tank, and camping gear strapped to the rear

Soft or hard Luggage?

Soft

Pros	Cons
Cheaper	Tricky waterproofing
Easy to store	Not so smart
Quick to fit	Not so protective

Hard

Pros	Cons
Smarter	Can be expensive
Usually waterproof	Wide panniers inhibit filtering
More capacious	Heavy
Better security	

Loading up

Loading the bike sounds like simplicity itself, but getting it right will make life on the road much easier. How well a bike handles is hugely affected by weight distribution, and ideally your luggage should be mounted as low as possible, and within the wheelbase. That's why many overland travellers use tank panniers, slung either side of the fuel items, or mount heavy stuff like spare fuel low down beside the engine. A badly loaded bike will feel like a drunken camel (not that I've ever ridden one of those, but you get the idea).

With standard bike luggage, place heavy items in the bottom of the panniers (unless it's something you need to get at several times a day), with lighter, bulkier stuff such as clothing on top. A topbox, being higher up, should only be used for less heavy items anyway. The tankbag is an ideal receptacle for valuables such as documents and cameras, as most can be unclipped/unzipped and carried around with you.

If camping, you'll almost certainly be strapping tent

ON THE ROAD

and sleeping bags on top of the rest of your luggage – it's amazing how 'compact' sleeping bags can fill a capacious pannier. Bungees are cheap and cheerful, and those multi-bungee cargo nets come highly recommended, though mini straps are more secure.

It's good to get into a routine of packing/unpacking the bike, keeping everything in the same place. You'd be surprised how much easier this makes life, especially if you're stopping in a different place every night.

Keep it accessible
Anything you need on a daily basis should be kept in a day-pack or tankbag – paperwork, a bottle of water, toothbrush, camera, a paperback, map and so on. Keep it light though. Night gear should be in an easily accessible grab-bag too, which makes for hassle-free night ferry crossings, B&Bs etc.

25

Loading needs care. Get into a routine of keeping everything in its place, and you'll save many minutes of frustrating searches

Having the right clothing is vital to having a good trip. This couple have a good combination of leather boots and jeans, plus waterproof Gore-Tex type jackets. Pack lighter clothes as well, for evenings and days off the bike

Clothing

Motorcycle clothing, like luggage, needs careful consideration, as it will determine your comfort and protection for the week, or month, or year that you're on the road. The first thing to do is get a good idea of the sort of climate you're heading for. Weather is never guaranteed, but forewarned is forearmed. Unless you're contemplating a trip in the autumn or winter, extreme cold can be discounted in Europe.

For wear on the bike, leather and Gore-Tex type fabrics each have their pros and cons. Leather is still the ultimate protective gear, though it's less flexible than fabric and, with one or two exceptions, isn't waterproof either, so to be sure of keeping dry you need to take a one-piece oversuit as well. If you do prefer leather, a two-piece suit is more adaptable than a one-piece, which can be torture on a hot day in southern Spain.

For touring abroad, breathable fabric jackets and trousers are far more comfortable and adaptable than leather. Being both waterproof and breathable, they're more pleasant to wear in hot, humid or downright wet weather. They're also lighter and more flexible than leather, and thus easier to walk around in – however keen you are on riding, you won't be spending all your time on the bike. The latest fabrics also have lightweight armour built in, so they're quite protective as well.

Similarly, your leather bike boots need to be comfortable enough to walk about in, all day if need be. If not, you'll need to squeeze a light pair of shoes into the luggage. Gloves should be waterproof, but if you insist on lightweight leather gloves that aren't, then take a spare pair – there's nothing worse than pulling on cold, soggy gloves first thing in the morning. As to helmets, the flip-up type is a good compromise, giving almost as much protection as a

ON THE ROAD

full-face with an open-face option for talking or just taking some fresh air.

Even if you're planning on being away for several weeks, there's no need to take a mountain of spare clothing, which will eat into your precious luggage room. Better to take fewer items and either find a launderette or wash them in your hotel room. Your bike gear, two sets of spare underwear and lightweight trousers to wear off the bike should do it. Go for multiple thin layers rather than heavy, chunky pullovers. These make for better insulation, trapping warm air between each layer. It's also easier to adjust your temperature by adding/removing layers.

Route planning

If there's a theme to this book, it's that the sort of trip you end up doing depends almost entirely on the sort of riding you want to do, and this is never more true than of route planning. Some bikers don't plan at all, but just head off the ferry and take pot luck, but most of us head for a particular region and then please ourselves when we get there.

If you want to just get there, then it's motorway time, and Europe in particular has a comprehensive network of well-maintained motorways. They tend to

The right trousers 27
The bike gear you already have will probably do the job, so you shouldn't have to rush out to invest in loads of new kit. But take a close look at where you're going and when. If it's going to be cold, then there's nothing so blissful as a heated waistcoat to back up your heated handgrips. Wimpy? Not at all; it's common sense.

Happiness is... two-up on the road to Paris, but it helps if you have decent maps and spend a bit of time on route planning. Motorways are quick and efficient, but you can miss a lot along the way

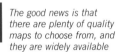

The good news is that there are plenty of quality maps to choose from, and they are widely available

be quieter than those in the UK, so can be a less stressful first leg of the journey if this is your first ride abroad. On the other hand, you can miss a lot on a motorway, and if you want to see the countryside it makes more sense to stick to the smaller roads – such as the lovely D roads of France – and accept that you'll take a bit longer to reach your destination.

A good map is essential. You won't have room for a big-format road atlas, but Michelin maps are excellent: compact, and with plenty of detail. The biker-friendly A5 atlases are small enough to squeeze into a tankbag (though the scale is less comprehensive) and some are even waterproof.

A more expensive option is the GPS (Global Positioning System), at around £400 for the basic unit, plus accessories. Not cheap, but a bike-specific GPS can tell you where you are, and work out the shortest or quickest route to where you want to be. It works by comparing the time it takes to receive signals from satellites orbiting the earth, which allows the GPS to pinpoint its position to within a few metres. This enables it to give continuous on-screen directions, though bikers are recommended to use an audio hook-up, which will work through a standard bike intercom. As the whole of Europe can be stored on two CDs, GPS is also a lot more compact than taking a series of maps. Some riders swear by GPS – others dream about what else they could do with £400. Take your pick.

Plan B
Something else that applies if you are heading for more remote areas. Rivers wash out, borders close, riots happen, as do accidents. Plan B will give you something to fall back on if your original plan becomes untenable. Like insurance, even if you never need it it's nice to know it's there.

ON THE ROAD

Navigation

However adept you are at finding your way around Britain, route finding abroad can still be confusing. Signs may not be as clear, and may give a local destination instead of the major one, or just the road number with no destination name at all (this system is used in the USA, with just the road number and its compass direction).

A good tip in French towns is to follow the *Toutes Directions* signs – these will take you out of town, where you'll be able to pick up signposts to your specific destination. European integration has given 'E' numbers to all major European roads, with even numbers running west/east and odd numbers north/south. This should make navigation across borders easier – look out for the green and white signs. Not all countries have entered into the spirit of E roads though – Britain's major roads have E numbers, but they're not signed as such.

Navigating on a motorcycle is more tricky than by car. It's obviously a bad idea for the rider to try and map-read on the move, but there are ways round it. One handy piece of kit is a translucent map holder that attaches to the rider's back, which the pillion can read to give directions on the move. It works better still if you have an intercom, for vocal directions. If riding solo, you've got no alternative but to stop and consult the map – a tankbag with a translucent map pocket is the most convenient accessory.

Buy good maps
Buy the best maps you can find. They'll repay you not only in planning a good route, but will show off-the-beaten-track sights that others will cruise on by. The evergreen Michelin maps are highly recommended, and highlight the scenic roads with a green line. Use a road atlas to get there, and a more local map once you arrive.

29

If in doubt about the route, stop and check, whether it's on the map or the GPS

One nice thing about riding abroad is how many more two-wheelers there are around, especially in cities. In many European towns, scooters are part of the urban fabric, so there are more parking facilities

Avoiding congestion

Not such a problem for motorcyclists, but even if you can filter slowly past traffic jams, it's still not much fun compared to breezing along an open road. So when route planning, try to avoid major cities at rush hour and at the start and end of weekends. The first two weeks of August are peak holiday time in Europe, especially in France, where the autoroutes heading out of Paris are likely to be at a standstill. Other hotspots are heading towards the ski resorts during the Alpine season, and border crossings in and out of the EU. But even if you do hit congestion, be thankful for one thing – you're not sitting in a car.

Ferries

If you live in Britain, and want to take your bike abroad, you'll have to take a ferry (unless you opt for Le Shuttle – see below). Ferries can take us to Germany, Ireland, Belgium, Spain, Denmark, Sweden, Norway, the Faeroe Islands, and even Iceland, as well as just across the Channel.

Taking a ferry can be quite daunting for novices, but there's no need to be nervous. In fact, ferries offer the advantage of some free time between the UK and overseas legs of the journey, allowing you to relax for a while. If you have a long ride on the other side, then taking an overnight ferry and booking a cabin is highly recommended. It allows you to start off in unfamiliar territory fresh and alert, and you don't need to worry about finding somewhere to stay immediately. There are cheaper alternatives to cabins, such as shared couchettes and reclining chairs, but no prizes for guessing which delivers the best night's sleep.

You'll need to book the ferry well in advance during peak season, though one advantage of being on a bike is that if you do miss your sailing, they can normally squeeze you onto the next one. Otherwise, it's a case of turning up about an hour before the boat leaves and riding into the numbered lane as directed – bikes are normally waved to the front of the lane, rather than sitting behind a queue of cars. Some ferry companies take the bikes on first, others make us wait – first on usually means first off as well, which is a bonus.

Ferry loading ramps are a slippery menace to motorcyclists, with a mixture of seawater, oil and diesel giving them all the grip of a well-worn manhole cover. Just be very gentle with the brakes (especially the front) and be aware that there may not be much grip when you put your feet down. On board, you'll be directed to a suitable space before

Plan and be flexible

Planning your trip beforehand (routes, where to stay and so on) is always worthwhile, but be flexible as well. You might decide to stay an extra night or two in an area you've fallen in love with, or even extend the trip by a few days. As long as your ferry ticket and work commitments allow, why not?

31

Ferries need booking in advance in the summer, and give a real sense of occasion to the start of any trip, whether you're heading for northern France or southern Africa

Metal ferry ramps need great care on a bike, as they will invariably be slippery from a mixture of sea water and oil. Just take it easy, and brake gently

the bike is tied down. In the past, ferry companies left riders to do this themselves, but increasingly the crew now do it for you, with proper straps instead of a length of oily old rope. But this varies depending on the company and whether the crew has time, so be prepared to tie the bike down yourself. The simplest way to do it is to bring a couple of mini ratchet straps. If the bike is on the sidestand, leave it in gear, and always strap it to something solid.

Even if the crossing is overnight, there's no need to struggle up to the top deck with all your gear. The tankbag, with your valuables, washing gear and a decent book, will be enough. Your helmet will be safe enough, locked to the bike. If you're on a budget, take your own food, as ferry restaurants have a captive market, and charge accordingly.

Crossing the Channel from Dover or Folkestone is the shortest and by far the most popular route to mainland Europe, but if you live in the west it might make more sense to head for the Poole, Portsmouth or Plymouth ferries. Arriving in Roscoff or Cherbourg, these make more sense if you're visiting western France or Spain. Or there's the overnight boat to Santander in northern Spain, which saves the long ride down through France. Another alternative which avoids long miles in the saddle is the Motorail service from Calais. This takes bikes as well as cars, and runs down to the south of France overnight, with connections to other parts of Europe.

Whichever ferry you decide to take, there's one pleasure that's unique to travelling by sea. Bike tied down, cabin located, you nip up on deck, lean over the rail and watch the White Cliffs drift into the distance – a perfect start to a riding holiday.

Le Shuttle

The alternative to ferries is Le Shuttle, which offers a quicker but less scenic route to France. You can just turn up and pay at the gate, but it's cheaper (and advisable in peak season, if you want to avoid a long wait) to book in advance. When Le Shuttle was planned, there was talk of special rest rooms for motorcyclists, but the reality is that you have to stand next to your bike for the 30-minute journey, or sit on the floor. There's also no means of tying it down (though they will bring out a front wheel clamp if you ask), so leave the bike in gear and stay close in case it falls over.

Passport control is on the UK side, so once on French soil you just ride out of the carriage and away. And that's Le Shuttle's main advantage over the ferry – speed.

World of biking
"Colin McRae the rally driver has a navigator, and so do I – my wife! We use an intercom, so that she can give me directions in advance, which is great when riding through unfamiliar cities."
Peter Avard

Le Shuttle is a quick and convenient means of crossing the Channel, but not quite so scenic as the ferry!

Intercoms

Communication, or lack of it, is one big drawback of motorcycling. Things that are so easy for a car driver and passenger – pointing out a good view, or suggesting a lunch stop at the auberge you've just passed – are reduced to a series of frantic shouts and hand signals.

But an intercom allows rider and pillion to talk normally at up to motorway speeds, with the option

A good intercoms system will greatly enhance two-up riding, make direction finding easier and the whole trip more of a shared experience – it needs careful setting up though

of music, a GPS input or the ability to receive hands-free phone calls. Having such a system can transform long-distance riding for a couple who want to really share the experience, though intercoms need to be set up carefully to give best performance. They're especially useful when the pillion acts as navigator – giving directions through an unfamiliar city, for example – and also prevent rider or pillion from getting lonely!

There are several different makes of intercom available, and everything from a basic music/phone set-up for rider only to a fully-loaded blue-tooth system for rider/pillion. Prices start at around £100, but expect to pay over £400 for a blue-tooth set-up. All the rider/pillion systems are based on a black box of electronics, plus two microphone/earpiece sets, and most use VOX (voice-activated operation) – that is, the microphone is automatically switched on when you start speaking. If the mike was on all the time, it would simply transmit wind blast through the earpieces continuously!

When setting up an intercom, both microphone and earpieces have to be positioned very carefully if the system is to be useable at speed. Using a modern intercom is simplicity itself, though you're connected to the bike and each other by leads. Even this can be avoided with one of the wire-free blue-tooth systems, though these are currently very new on the market.

The basic intercom hardware can also be used to power a bike-to-bike system, in conjunction with suitable radios. These have a range of up to two miles, and are useful for keeping a group of riders together, even if they're out of sight of each other.

Intercom Talk

VOX: Voice-activated operation. The microphone only switches on when you talk, to block out wind blast when you're not. VOX does this automatically.

PTT: Push to talk. As above, the microphone is only switched on while you're talking, but in this case it's activated by a thumb button on the bars.

Noise cancelling: A system that enables the microphone to recognise desirable sounds (your voice) and cut out undesirable sounds (wind blast and engine roar).

ON THE ROAD

Safe riding

Motorcycling, as we are constantly reminded, is a dangerous activity, but the danger can be minimised by riding defensively. It's worth remembering that the vast majority of road crashes involve rider or driver error, so concentrating on the ride will dramatically improve your safety.

This is doubly important when riding abroad. We might think that British car drivers can be dull-witted, aggressive and/or unable to 'think bike', but on an international scale they're not too bad. Britain has one of the lowest vehicle death rates in the world. Not that this is any cause for complacency, but the fact remains that accident rates are higher abroad. Ride into the developing world, and they soar.

If you haven't already taken an advanced riding course, do so. These range from full week-long residential courses to an observed assessment ride of an hour or two. Even an assessment ride will indicate any weak spots you need to work on, and any form of advanced training will always improve your riding. Not only that, but advanced riding skills learnt in the UK will pay exactly the same dividends when riding abroad, however unfamiliar the surroundings.

The basics of good riding amount to little more than common sense, but they're worth repeating. The more time and space you have to react to situations, the more likely you are to avoid an accident. Anticipation and reading the road ahead are key to this. Look beyond the car just ahead of you, and anticipate problems before you're on top of them.

Be ready for unfamiliar road layouts in advance, so that you're in the right lane when you reach them. Slow down well in advance, and keep a two-second gap between you and the car in front (double that in poor weather). Drivers in a foreign country may react differently to the way you expect, so hang back and check what their intentions are. Just like riding at home, your safety is your own responsibility, so don't rely on other drivers to do the right thing. Finally, don't ride when you're tired – this could be fatal.

Road casualties worldwide
Deaths annually per 10,000 motor vehicles

Norway	1.1
Switzerland	1.4
UK	1.5
Australia	1.8
Germany	1.9
United States	2.0
New Zealand	2.2
France	2.6
Spain	2.9
Ireland	3.4
Portugal	4.8
Thailand	9.0
South Africa	17.0
India	20.0
Venezuela	58.0
Kenya	64.0

Not an invitation to freestyle riding, but a warning of bumps in the road. Despite international agreements, road signs won't always be familiar

Keeping to the right isn't such a worry for UK bikers as it is for car drivers, as you can still use the width of the lane to maximise visibility

Overtaking needs special care abroad. Pay attention to no-overtaking signs (above) and road markings. Many countries use a single solid white line to prohibit overtaking in both directions, unlike the double solid white line we have in the UK

World of biking
"When riding abroad, I tape a little message – 'Keep Right' – onto the handlebars, just below the ignition key. That way I'm reminded of it whenever I climb back on the bike, after filling up with fuel or stopping to look at the view."
Jim Skellern

Riding on the right
At least there's one thing you won't need to worry about – using right-hand-drive on the 'wrong' side of the road. When riding on the right, a bike can make use of the road space to maximise visibility, just as you would at home. It's also more natural than you might think, as traffic, road signs and marks will constantly remind you to keep right.

The first day isn't usually the problem, as most of us are keyed up to riding on the right after rolling off the ferry, but it's still a good idea to make those first few kilometres straightforward – use a motorway rather than plunging straight into a busy city centre. Mistakes more often happen a few days into the trip, after you've had a chance to relax. Watch out for deceptively simple manoeuvres, such as pulling out onto the road after filling up with fuel, or turning out of a side-turning. U-turns also need great care, as do narrow roads with no white line to remind you.

Repeating the mantra 'Think Right – Look Left' will help, especially when you're about to pull out on to the road. Ask your pillion to remind you whenever you set off. Apart from the few countries that drive on the left (none, UK excepted, in Europe) the golden rule is 'keep right'.

Overtaking
Another advantage for motorcyclists over drivers of right-hand-drive cars is that your overtaking visibility is unaffected by riding on the right, though the whole manoeuvre will be a mirror image of the familiar one at home. Otherwise, all the same rules apply: avoid overtaking near junctions and crossroads, and before

committing yourself be absolutely sure that you can return to your side of the road safely. Overtaking on the left is one of those things that feels odd at first, but you get used to it.

Some countries, such as Sweden and Ireland, have a hard shoulder even on two-lane roads, and it's usual for slow vehicles to move over and let you pass. Many European drivers will pull over a little anyway, to allow a bike past. Always acknowledge such courtesy with a wave of your left hand once past. Wouldn't it be nice if M25 commuters were that considerate? Some countries also expect the overtaking driver/rider to flash headlights or sound the horn before accelerating past, so this isn't necessarily a sign or aggression.

Overtaking on the inside is illegal in Britain on motorways and dual-carriageways, unless the traffic in the outside lane is in a queue, and the same rule applies in most other countries. But there's no such rule in the United States, where overtaking on either side is acceptable on multi-lane highways. Drivers are supposed to stick to the inside lane when not overtaking, but in practice many stay in the middle lane to avoid being channelled off at an exit, when the inside lane becomes a compulsory exit lane. So changing lanes on an interstate needs extra care, especially when pulling back on to the inside lane: someone could be overtaking you there at speed.

Learn the rules
Wherever you're going, take the time to learn the rules of the road, which may be formalised or may just be local etiquette. In Italy, no one seems to use their mirrors, and the time they save means that driving is done at almost demonic speed. In South Africa, you pull to the left to let faster cars go by. On American freeways you can overtake on either side.

37

Right or left?
We may be outnumbered by European countries driving on the right, but Britain is by no means the only place where drivers still stick to the left. Other left-hand-drivers include:
Australia
Cyprus
India
Japan
Kenya
Malaysia
Malta
Mauritius
Mozambique
Namibia
South Africa
Tanzania
Thailand
New Zealand

Riding through an unfamiliar town needs concentration, so it's better to leave navigation to your pillion, if possible

Indicator signals, unlike headlight flashes, mean the same everywhere, only the custom and practice of where and when to use them varies. If in doubt, use them

World of biking

UK bikers often come home with the impression that European riders are more friendly, because just about all of them wave to other riders, a tradition that is dying out in Britain. They could be inherently more friendly, or it could be that riding on the right leaves your left (offside) hand free, making it easier to wave. In Britain, our offside hand is usually busy hanging on to the twistgrip.

Signalling

Clear use of your indicators is vital, whether riding through Birmingham or Brindisi – as in just about every area of life, vagueness brings misunderstanding, and you don't want that while circulating an unfamiliar roundabout.

When abroad, you're likely to be approaching road layouts more slowly than the locals, so it's essential to give a clear indication of what you intend to do. Even if the norm is not to indicate in a given situation, if there's any doubt or hesitation in your manoeuvre use of the indicators should make things clear.

Custom and practice varies between countries. Indicators are often used late during manoeuvres in Britain, but German drivers tend to be more disciplined. American drivers are at the opposite extreme, and often don't indicate at all, which makes things extra uncertain on the highways, where overtaking on both sides is permitted. So be ready for the car in front to change lanes without apparent warning. Other countries are more stringent than Britain, with a legal requirement to indicate when returning to your own side of the road after overtaking.

Headlight flashing is another signal that can cause confusion. It Britain, it means 'I'm giving way to you'. But in France it means the exact opposite: 'Give way, I'm coming through' – a potentially dangerous misunderstanding. So if someone does flash you, hang back and make absolutely sure of their intentions before carrying on. Drivers with a personal vendetta against speed limits sometimes use the headlight flash to warn of speed traps, but don't expect this to be the case everywhere.

ON THE ROAD

Right of way

Priorité au droite – give way to the right – is the rule in many countries, not just France. It simply means that traffic emerging from the right automatically has priority, even if turning from a side street onto a major road. Unless, that is, there's an indication to the contrary. This is shown by a yellow diamond sign on the road that has priority over all roads joining it.

If there's no yellow diamond (or if the sign has three diagonal black lines through it, indicating the end of the priority zone) be prepared for cars to shoot out of right-hand side turnings, expecting you to give way, especially in rural France.

The horn

Few aspects of road behaviour are more varied than use of the horn. In Britain it's hardly used at all, except as a rebuke, which of course is the worst possible motive. Otherwise, a national reticence seems to discourage us from even giving a gentle toot where it would be appropriate.

Whatever country you're riding in, the horn has just one meaning – to let other road users know that you're there. Some European drivers use it in just that way, to let you know they're about to overtake for example. In the Third World and in Southern Europe, the slightest hold up in traffic is a sign for communal honking. It's not aggression, but just the way they do things. But don't be tempted to join in, as regulations are being tightened – it's better to be a reticent Brit tourist than the recipient of a hefty fine.

A yellow diamond sign means that the road you are on has priority over all roads joining it. When this sign is cancelled (below) you must be prepared to give way to traffic joining from the right, even from a minor road

Horn etiquette varies from country to country, and isn't necessarily a sign of aggression. Don't let British good manners stop you from letting traffic know that you're there

Motorways will get you places fast and efficiently, but you can miss out on some great countryside and twisty tarmac. Be prepared to pay a toll in some countries, and make sure you've got enough fuel to make the next service area

World of biking
Joining a French motorway, I stopped at the booth, but it failed to deliver a ticket. I waited as the queue of cars built up behind me. It was impossible to do a U-turn and try again, so I parked the bike on the hard shoulder and jogged back to the booth, walked through as a pedestrian... and it worked! Not recommended at busy booths, though.

Motorways
After Britain's congested motorways, some of those in the rest of Europe can seem like a dream come true. Most of the Continent has a network of well maintained motorways, and most countries have more of them than in the UK as well. As a result, outside commuter rush hours and holiday hotspots they're often lightly trafficked.

For motorcyclists, motorways aren't the most exciting roads to travel on, but they will at least allow you to cover long distances relatively quickly. They're also safer than smaller roads, as all traffic is heading in the same direction at a similar speed. However, you often have to pay for the privilege of using them, as on the French *péage*, which can add up if you're doing a lot of motorway miles. The system is quite simple. You take a ticket at the automated toll booth when joining the motorway – don't use the booths signed tele*péage*, as these are for season ticket holders only. Keep the ticket somewhere safe, preferably an inside pocket, as if you can't find it at the other end they'll charge you the maximum fee. When you exit the motorway you have to stop at a manned booth, hand over your ticket, and they'll tell you how much to pay. Wherever it is, have a handful of change or your credit card ready, to avoid holding up a queue of traffic – the quickest way to pay tolls is for your pillion to take care of the whole process.

ON THE ROAD

Some countries, such as Switzerland and Austria, impose a blanket motorway tax instead of individual tolls. To use motorways in these countries you need to buy a special tax disc called a vignette, and have it ready for inspection.

Foreign motorways are often different from British motorways in other ways too. Signposting is sometimes not so far in advance of slip roads as in the UK, so be ready to move into the inside lane as early as you can. The slip roads themselves can have tighter curves than we're used to, with all the usual hazards of diesel and oil spillages, so slow down well in advance. As a warning, speed limit signs are often posted on the slip road.

High speed
It's become a truism that Britain is not the place for high speed riding any more, with its 70mph limit and latest generation of speed cameras. With even 600cc sports bikes capable of over 160mph, and legends like the Suzuki Hayabusa close to 200mph, the prospect of clearer roads on the Continent is a tempting one.

It is true that several European countries have higher motorway speed limits than we do. The limit in France and Austria is 130kph (81mph), and some Italian motorways now allow up to 150kph (93mph). But even in Germany, the famous absence of a speed limit only applies to certain sections, and even these have a recommended limit of 130kph (81mph) and less than that past service areas, in poor weather, or through roadworks.

If you do head for the Autobahn intent on exploiting your bike's full potential, there are some things you need to be aware of:

♦ Many stretches of Autobahn have only two lanes and feature relatively sharp bends, despite the lack of a speed limit. The corners will be easy at 70mph, but turn into something quite scary at twice that speed.

Within range
Know what your bike's fuel range is, at motorway and non-motorway speeds. Use the tripmeter (even if you've got a fuel gauge) to remind you when you'll next need to stop for fuel, and zero it every time you fill up.

Ahh, speed. Riding abroad can give the chance to indulge in higher speed riding than in the UK, because of lower traffic levels or higher speed limits

♦ Stopping distances increase dramatically with speed, even if your bike has race spec calipers. It takes almost three times as far to stop from 120mph as from 70mph. In the wet of course, it takes even longer.

♦ However fast you're riding, a Porsche-driving local is likely to come up behind you on full beam, expecting you to pull over and allow him past. Don't be tempted to follow: keen Germans often have plenty of experience of driving at three-figure speeds, more than the rest of us.

♦ Your bike may be capable of cruising at well over 100mph, but it needs to be in tip-top condition to do so. Tyres, chain and brakes should all be as good as they can be. Check the handbook: you may also need to set higher tyre pressures than normal.

♦ Fuel consumption soars at high speed, so be sure you've got enough juice to reach the next service area.

♦ After riding at high speed, take time to wind down, acclimatising yourself to lower speeds before rejoining normal roads. Speedometers do lie sometimes, but they still give more realistic information than your speed-attuned senses.

ON THE ROAD

Driving styles

Italians drive fast and flamboyantly, Germans are arrogant but disciplined, Indians chaotic, and Scandinavians tend to be the most law-abiding in the world. National stereotypes, perhaps, but there's no denying that driving styles, and attitudes to safety, do vary wildly across the world. Whatever we think of British drivers, there are plenty of others with a more cavalier mindset on the road. According to one survey, three-quarters of Italian drivers felt that motorists should be free to decide how much they can drink before driving. Only one-fifth of Swedish drivers agreed.

Statements about national or regional driving can only ever amount to generalisations, but it's true that in Southern Europe, for example, motorists tend to drive faster. It's a particular surprise for motorcyclists who are used to making good progress on UK roads. Overtaking is faster and more frequent, even occurring on blind bends, so you just need to be ready to meet an oncoming driver on your side of the road. Like the enthusiastic use of the horn, this isn't necessarily a sign of aggression or road rage, just the way things are done. Of course, it's also the reason why Portugal and Greece have a road fatality rate three times that of Britain.

Slower local drivers will often accommodate the overtakers by moving over to let them pass (from whichever direction), and you need to do the same. If someone pulls over for you, make absolutely sure it's safe to pass before going for it. Other behaviour of foreign drivers – tailgating on Italian motorways, or the apparent impatience of French drivers in town – is undeniably dangerous, and to us might seem to be rude and aggressive. But it's just the way things are done, and flashing or gesticulating at such drivers is often counterproductive.

Motorcycling abroad doesn't mean you have to ride just like the locals do. Just be aware that their habits will often be different from yours.

Be friendly
Take time to talk to the locals, and they'll invariably respond in kind. In Third World countries people may be scared of someone swathed in bike kit, so a flip-up helmet will help. A smile and a handshake go a long way to breaking the ice, but if you haven't taken the time to learn about the customs of the people whose country you're travelling through, you can have a miserable and abrasive time.

43

Take regular breaks, have a drink and stretch your legs. This will keep you relaxed and keep fatigue at bay for longer

Fatigue

Tiredness can be fatal on a bike, as you often don't realise how tired you are until you stop, or until it's too late. Drivers do fall asleep at the wheel – it's thought that one in five motorway accidents are caused by just that – and motorcyclists are human too.

Riding abroad makes you especially vulnerable to fatigue. It's exciting, but also stressful, thanks to the long hours in the open, and the unfamiliar roads and surroundings. On top of that, you'll often be riding longer distances than usual, perhaps with the temptation to squeeze more miles out of each day. It all adds up to a perfect recipe for rider fatigue.

So don't be tempted to ride into the night to make up distance. It's better to find somewhere to stay and make an early start. Be wary of medicines that can cause drowsiness, such as some cold and flu remedies. Don't ride for more than two hours at a time, and have a break of at least 15 minutes between stints. Walk around and use different muscles – this is just as refreshing as sitting down with a coffee, but make time for both. Unless your pillion can pilot the bike, you won't be able to share riding, so the rider's alertness is paramount.

Rest stops are frequent on most motorway networks in Europe (especially France), North America and

ON THE ROAD

Australia. If you do feel tired, stop, drink a strong coffee and allow yourself a 15-minute nap, stretched out on the grass – your pillion can watch things while you sleep. You should wake up as the caffeine starts to kick in, but the bottom line is to plan your journey and daily mileage so that you don't need to do this.

Filling up

Unleaded petrol is now the norm right across Europe, North America and Australia, though this shouldn't be an issue unless you're riding an old British classic, or a pre-1980s Japanese bike. Some modern bikes may still need 98 octane super unleaded, which is available across Europe but can't be counted on everywhere.

Filling stations may be self-service or attended, and credit cards are accepted just about everywhere, but it's as well to have some cash with you, just in case. A lot of American stations insist you pay the cashier before using the pump – you get a refund if the tank fills before you've had all that you've paid for. Wherever you are, it's a good idea to remove your helmet when walking in to pay – cashiers can be nervous of anonymous helmeted figures.

Do short days
Plan your days to be shorter than your instincts tell you. You might find 500-mile days a doddle on UK motorways, but on unfamiliar roads you'll have to concentrate harder and ride more slowly. Set ambitious targets, and you run the risk both of making mistakes to try and achieve them, and burning past things that you'll never see the like of again.

Colour-coded pumps make filling up easy across Europe, so there's very little danger of filling your tank with diesel ('Gazole' here) by mistake

ROAD
HAZARDS

Road hazards – junctions, traffic lights and roundabouts – are part of life on the road, but don't assume that these familiar features will be the same wherever you go. Subtle differences, such as the traffic light sequence, have a great affect on how you should approach them.

Other hazards are quite unlike anything we come across while biking in Britain. Wild elk and kangaroos aren't a particular problem on the A6, and the Mersey Tunnel isn't a patch on the tunnel that burrows through Mt Blanc.

Whatever the hazard, however familiar it might seem on the surface, always slow down and approach with care, giving yourself time to assess it properly.

Traffic light sequences vary across the world, but red only ever means one thing – stop

48

Traffic signs may be more familiar abroad than you expect. This Spanish 'no right turn' sign will be clear to any British rider, while the unique inverted triangle shape of the 'give way' sign reveals its meaning whatever language it's written in

Traffic signs

Traffic signs across much of the world – certainly in the countries you're likely to be riding in – are far easier to understand than you might think. This is thanks to the 1968 Vienna convention on road signs and signals, which agreed a general harmonisation of signs as follows:

▲ triangular signs **warn**

● circular signs **prohibit**

■ rectangular signs **inform**

ROAD **HAZARDS**

In addition, the octagonal 'stop' sign is universally recognised, as is the inverted triangle for 'give way'. To make things even easier (for us Brits), many road signs abroad are expressed in English. Not only is it the international language, but English lends itself to short, pithy phrases that are ideal for road signs. 'Give way' is less poetic than 'Cedéz le passage', but more to the point.

And thanks to that international usage of English, it is utilised even in countries which do not use the Roman alphabet. In Russia, Japan and Saudi Arabia, directional signs will often give the place name in English as well as in national characters.

Not that all these common standards should make us complacent, as there are still plenty of differences out there. Some signs, such as the yellow diamond indicating that traffic on that road has priority, are simply not found in Britain. Others will need translating – check the sections on individual countries in the back of this book, or have a pocket dictionary handy.

Traffic signs won't always be as large or clear as they are in Britain, and the colours can vary too – Italian motorway signs are green, for instance.

Road markings
More good news, as the general principles of road markings are the same all over the world. The more white paint there is on the road, the greater the hazard.

An unbroken white line at a junction means 'stop', and often even uses the English word – as with road signs, the language of Shakespeare lends itself to short, sharp messages. As in Britain, a 'stop' sign does not mean 'give way', even if the locals are creeping over it without coming to a complete halt. In fact, that goes for any traffic law that a local driver is obviously breaking. They may know what they can get away with, but you don't.

A single or double solid white line in the middle of the road means no crossing the line, just as it does in

Watch out for signs that look familiar but may not mean exactly what you expect. A sign warning of a right-hand bend in the road might indicate a more severe bend than you would expect if you encountered it in the UK

Handily enough for British bikers, the word 'stop' is an almost universal warning, although the configuration of junctions may still cause us a little confusion

Britain. The criteria used to apply solid lines varies from country to country, but it's not worth crossing one even if you think it's safe to overtake. Even if the road markings do permit overtaking, only commit yourself once you're convinced it's safe to do so.

Junctions

Most accidents occur at junctions, as every motorcyclist who has had a vehicle pull out in front of him/her from a side street will know. This danger is compounded abroad by unfamiliar junctions, which may not give a clear indication of who has priority. If there's no indication at all, then in most countries the priority is to give way to the right. The best advice is to take things slowly, and not be fazed if traffic suddenly appears from an unexpected direction. If in doubt, stop and give yourself a couple of seconds of orientation time.

Crossroads can cause particular confusion, especially when there's no indication of priority. In the US, priority goes to whoever reaches the stop line first, or from the right if two vehicles get there at the same time. When you want to turn across oncoming traffic, and an approaching vehicle wants to do the same, the British recommendation is to pass around the back of each other, to avoid obscuring the view of oncoming traffic. In Italy, the rule insists that you pass in front of each other.

Some European countries (Spain, for example) give a refuge on the right-hand side of two-lane main roads. Traffic turning left is expected to wait there instead of in the middle of the road – it may take longer, but it's probably safer.

In Italy, if you intend to turn across another vehicle you must pass in front of it, not behind

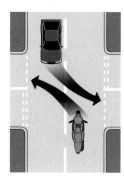

Roundabouts

Britain used to be almost unique in its love of roundabouts, and the system that gave traffic on the roundabout priority. On much of the Continent, the opposite rule applied – traffic on the roundabout had to give way to that entering it.

Most European roundabouts have now switched to the British system, and in France drivers are reminded by signs stating *Vous n'avez pas priorité* (you do not have priority) or *Cedéz le passage* (give way). The old rule has hung on for some rural roundabouts, so don't assume anything. Oddly, the massive roundabout around the Arc de Triomphe in Paris still uses the old system as well. If you can cope with this cobble stoned monster at rush hour, you have nothing else to fear.

Roundabouts are far less common in the United States, where they are called traffic circles or rotaries. In this case, the American driver may be just as confused as you, so take care.

51

There are roundabouts (called 'rotaries') in America too, but they are few and far between

Extra care is needed on roundabouts, as in some countries vehicles entering the roundabout may have priority over those which are already on it.

Red lights means stop wherever you are, but there can be differences in the colour sequence, in filtering law, and how much notice local drivers pay to traffic lights

In Australia, a stop sign with three black dots on it means that if the traffic lights are out of order or flashing amber, you must stop and give way to traffic as if at a junction controlled by a stop sign

Traffic lights

Wherever you ride, you are likely to find traffic lights, and they serve exactly the same function as they do in Britain. The difference lies in the detail, and the extent to which drivers actually obey them.

The lights may be a different shape or size to the ones we're used to in Britain, mounted at a different height or hung from a wire strung across the road. So you have to be vigilant, especially when driving through an unfamiliar town or city, where you're certain to find traffic lights. One common feature (and a really good idea which has never caught on in the UK) is a small set of repeater lights, fixed to the traffic light pole at head height, so if you're first in the queue you're not craning your head up to keep the main lights in view.

The actual light sequence may be different as well, and in fact most countries go straight from red to green, missing out the red-and-amber stage altogether. Be ready for this, unless you want to provoke a cacophony of hooting. The continuously flashing amber light means you can proceed as long as the junction is clear, but you still have to give way to other vehicles or pedestrians.

Some North American and Canadian traffic lights (but none in New York or Quebec) allow traffic to turn right against a red light, after first stopping to check that it's safe to go. Where this doesn't apply, there should be a sign prohibiting it. Some European countries have adopted the right turn on red rule at some traffic lights – in Germany, a green arrow indicates where this is permitted.

British traffic lights faithfully carry on their familiar sequence 24 hours a day, but in some countries the

ROAD **HAZARDS**

pattern changes at night. In the US, a flashing amber light means slow down and exercise caution, but you don't need to stop; flashing red means stop and check before riding on. Some lights in Germany are actually turned off overnight, in which case the give way or stop signs will show you what's expected.

Despite the rules, American drivers aren't averse to cruising past red lights – this caused 89,000 crashes in 1998, and nearly 1,000 deaths, a staggering figure. So the old advice stays true even if you have a green light: look right-left-right as you approach a crossroads, just in case the guy coming the other way is late for work and doesn't intend to stop. Green means go – if the way is clear.

By the same token, where drivers have a more 'flexible' approach to traffic lights, be aware that the tailgating driver behind you may not expect you to stop when the lights turn red. Slow down well in advance, and use your brake light to make it clear that you're a cautious tourist. He might curse you under his breath, but he's less likely to rear-end your bike.

Pedestrian crossings

Etiquette at pedestrian crossings varies across the world. The British are a relatively polite bunch, usually stopping at a zebra crossing if someone is waiting to cross. Many other countries take a different line, and vehicles aren't expected to stop – it's up to the pedestrian to wait until the road is clear, even on a designated crossing. Despite this, pedestrians can be fined for failing to use that crossing, or for walking across against a red light. The upshot is that following drivers may not expect you to stop and let pedestrians cross.

The best advice is to ride slowly, and take note of what the locals do – you should have a good idea after your first trip through a town centre. In Japan, drivers and riders turning into a side street are expected to give pedestrians crossing that street right of way.

53

World of Biking
"In Milan, traffic lights are instructions. In Rome, they are suggestions. In Naples, they are Christmas decorations."
Antonio Martino, Italian Defence Minister

The sequence and meaning of traffic light signals abroad can differ from those used in the UK

In many countries drivers do not stop to give way to pedestrians waiting at a zebra crossing. If you do decide to stop, check your mirrors first or you risk being rear-ended by a surprised local motorist

Railway crossings

Railway level crossings, especially in rural backwaters, may not have the automatic gates that we're used to. There may be flashing lights to warn of a train coming, but sometimes you won't even find these – unprotected crossings are a feature of some of the more remote parts of the US. The drill is to stop and make absolutely sure there's no train coming (sounds obvious…). If in doubt, switch off your engine, or get your pillion to hop off and wave you across.

Tunnels

Riding through tunnels can be quite spectacular, if you're used to the average British road tunnel. We don't have enough mountains to make big tunnels worthwhile for road engineers.

Many tunnels and motorways abroad have minimum as well as maximum speed limits. The minimum permitted speed is indicated by a number in a blue circle

Contrast this with some of the motorways that follow Italy's undulating coastline, traversing a constant succession of bridges and tunnels. They make the M62 look pretty tame. In the Alps, some road tunnels are true feats of engineering. Take the St Gothard in Switzerland, the world's longest at 16km (10 miles) – it's also 1,000m above sea level. There's something surreal about riding in this artificial darkness for 15-20 minutes, while it's bright and sunny outside.

But such long tunnels bring their own dangers. Plunging from bright sunlight into darkness is disconcerting at first, so slow down and give your eyes time to adjust. Don't brake hard though, which invites a rear-end shunt – just ease off your speed as you approach the tunnel. Emerging into the bright sunlight can be just as disconcerting, but again, your eyes will adjust in a few seconds.

If you're not already using a dipped headlight, switch it on, even in brightly-lit tunnels – there are usually signs reminding you to do this. There is often a toll to pay on the longer tunnels.

There have been some horrific crashes in tunnels, with fires claiming a total of 50 lives in the St Gothard and Mt Blanc tunnels recently. If anything does happen, there's little space to take avoiding action, so keep well back from the vehicle in front, and slow down – both minimum and maximum speeds will be signed. If there is a crash, stop and head for the emergency exits, which will be clearly marked.

A few Alpine tunnels offer a rail shuttle service instead of a road – you just ride on, as you would on Le Shuttle, and ride off at the other end. A good idea if the alternative is slithering over a snow-covered pass.

World of biking
"I travelled to Canada by ship in the 1970s. After we'd docked very early one morning a whole group of us walked off the boat into downtown Vancouver, and, used to London traffic, dutifully obeyed the red stick man at the first pedestrian crossing we came to. A police car stopped and asked what on earth we were doing – we needn't worry about red lights at 4am when Vancouver roads were empty."
Anna Finch

Always put on your dipped headlamps when passing through a road tunnel. You must do this by law in most countries, whether or not the tunnel is lit

In parts of northen Europe, such as Holland and Denmark, you'll find far more cyclists than in the UK, but they tend to stick to cycle lanes and paths

Cyclists

Motorcyclists and cyclists don't normally come into conflict – we share the same hazards of British weather, dodgy road surfaces and drivers apparently blind to two-wheeled traffic. Cyclists are also relatively rare in the UK, at least outside the major cities.

But things are different in many parts of northern Europe, especially Germany, the Netherlands, France and Denmark. Here, a less car-bound culture and networks of cycle paths and lanes encourage many more cyclists to take to the roads, so you have to be ready for them. Cycle lanes may also have priority over motor traffic, which needs watching. Finally, strength in numbers tends to make cyclists more confident, so don't expect them to ride in the gutter.

Perhaps the French have the right idea – anyone overtaking a cyclist has to leave a two-metre gap by law.

Scooters

Scooters, despite a recent drop in popularity, are still very much part of street life in southern Europe. Many are used by the young – expect to see plenty of helmetless youths in shorts and T-shirts, whipping in and out of the traffic to the accompaniment of a screaming two-stroke that hasn't seen a working silencer for some time. Don't try to follow these 'twist and go' scoots through narrow gaps on your big touring bike, and be ready for a thumbs-up as they pull up alongside you at the lights.

Many other scooter riders in Europe are matter-of-fact commuters, and it all works in your favour. The sheer number of two-wheelers on the roads creates an awareness of bikes that is lacking in British cities, except perhaps London. Once again, it's strength in numbers, and it's a good feeling.

ROAD **HAZARDS**

Trams

Unless you ride in Croydon or Glasgow, you probably won't have encountered a tram in Britain, but they're a common sight in many foreign cities. Trams should be treated with respect, as they can't take avoiding action if you get in the way, and can't stop as quickly as a bus.

The regulations vary, but trams usually have priority over other traffic, especially when pulling away from a stop. You are usually permitted to overtake trams on the right (the nearside) but you must always give way to passengers getting on and off. Crossing metal tramlines may need care in the wet as well.

Trams are a picturesque feature of cities such as Amsterdam (above); riders should take care not to obstruct them and give way where required

Cobbles, wet tramlines and not much room to manoeuvre, just some of the hazards to be seen on tram routes in Lubeck, northern Germany.

58

In the US, do not ride past a stationary school bus with its red lights flashing, even if you are on the other side of the road

School buses

Always ride with care at school time, and especially when passing school buses – except in the US, where you aren't permitted to overtake the familiar yellow bus at all when it is stopped with its red lights flashing, even if you're on the opposite side of the road. This rule even applies if you're on the other side of a multi-lane highway, though you don't have to stop if there's a central reservation, so long as you slow down. American police take this particular 'no overtaking' rule very seriously, so flout it at your peril.

Animals

Hitting a large animal is serious enough in a car, but on a motorcycle it's often fatal. In most of Europe, the largest four-legged creatures you're likely to find in the road (New Forest ponies aside) are sheep or goats, which are famously blessed with very little road sense. Even these are substantial enough to knock you off should you hit one. While eating, they're unlikely to run across the road, but they can panic at your approach. Slowing down, and constant vigilance, are the only answers – attempting to S-bend around them rarely works. Where there is one sheep or goat, there will be many more, so don't assume passing a couple means you're past the danger.

Large, heavier animals (often larger and heavier than you and your bike combined) are an even more serious hazard. In Scandinavia, elk can weigh up to half a tonne, and are apt to trot across the road without looking. Canadians call them moose, but the effect is the same. Be especially careful in wooded areas, especially if the trees run right up to the roadside – the narrower the verge, the less warning you have.

Australian cars in the Outback wear 'roo bars' for good reason, but motorcyclists have no such protection. The most dangerous time is at night, so take advantage of a few tinnies in the bar and a good night's sleep – never ride though the Outback in darkness.

ROAD **HAZARDS**

Minor roads in farming areas may be gated to keep stock in or out, so the golden rule is to leave the gate exactly as you found it: open if it was open, closed if it was closed. Gates are usually left open for a reason – to let stock get to a water supply, for example – so closing an open gate could have disastrous results. If there's a group of you, the lead bike should stop and wait by the gate, to ensure it is left as it was found.

There's plenty of wildlife in the National Parks of the US, and bears have become expert at breaking into cars looking for titbits, which means bikes are pretty vulnerable to a toothy assault. Don't leave any food on the bike, especially overnight – the smell will attract hirsute diners in search of a free lunch.

It's not just wild animals that can prove a hazard, and in many countries farmers still herd livestock along the road

Emergency vehicles

Most British drivers and riders will pull over to allow emergency vehicles past, and in some countries, such as the United States, this is a legal requirement. Other countries forbid following the police or ambulance too closely, or stopping near an emergency site. Military and state vehicles have the same status in some places too. In the United States, if you spot a phalanx of Harley-mounted outriders and a big black limousine, get well out of the way.

RULES AND REGULATIONS

Wherever you ride, there will be a multiplicity of rules to comply with. Most will be similar to those in the UK, but not all, so it makes sense to be ultra-vigilant when touring abroad.

You need to be on your best behaviour at all times, and just because local bikers are apparently flouting the law doesn't mean it's safe for you to do the same. With a foreign plate, you will actually be a more visible target to the police, so beware. As ever, ignorance of the law is no defence, so make sure you're familiar with local speed limits and regulations before you cross the border.

This chapter gives an overview of the situations you are likely to encounter, but for specific advice on individual countries consult the information at the back of this book.

61

Always expect the unexpected. Traffic rules have to be obeyed to the letter, whatever the locals appear to be getting away with, though these Spanish police probably have a very good reason for riding down steps

PRECAUCIÓN
A más velocidad
semáforo en rojo
50

The words on this sign might not be clear at first glance, but the graphics will be – this Spanish sign refers to a 50kph limit around the corner, enforced by traffic lights which turn red if you're breaking the limit

Speed limits

This is the age of the speed camera, radar detection and a general crackdown on speeding, so if you break the limit you're more likely to get caught than ever before.

Whatever you think of speed cameras, there's no denying that they've cut accidents and saved lives in the UK. In the Australian state of Victoria, a zero tolerance approach to speeding was highly unpopular at first, but the bottom line was a dramatic reduction in the number of crashes, deaths and injuries.

So speed limits work, but there's another reason for respecting them. Police forces in many parts of the world will levy a hefty on-the-spot fine on speeding tourists, and may even impound your bike as well. Sailing home on the ferry as a foot passenger, up to €2,000 the poorer, is not an appealing prospect, however great your need for speed.

The trouble is speed limits vary wildly across the world – check the sections on specific countries at the back of this book for the actual limits. Even within Europe there's a wide variation. Norway has a decidedly laidback open road limit of 90kph (55mph), but in Germany, you could theoretically ride your Honda Blackbird up the Autobahn at a flat-out 300kph (186mph) and not get into trouble.

In a way, bikers in the UK have it easy. Speed limit signs are large and clear, often with reinforcing signs painted on the road, while even speed cameras are painted bright yellow so that you can't miss them. Signs abroad won't necessarily be so easy to spot, and even if there's no sign as you approach a village, you have to assume that the urban limit starts with the village's name sign. Unless otherwise indicated, the sign at the other end of the village, with the name crossed out, can be taken as the end of the limit. In France, the rappel sign, seen periodically throughout urban areas, is a reminder that the limit is still in force.

Many countries impose a lower speed limit in poor weather – it's only advisory in Britain, but mandatory in France, where the motorway limit is lowered from

RULES AND REGULATIONS

130kph to 110kph when it's raining. Once again, don't be drawn along by locals apparently flouting the limit – it's not much of a defence if you get pulled over.

Even if you can't see an obvious police presence, don't assume there isn't one. American police use planes equipped with radar to spot speeders – if they catch you, a traffic cop in the next town will be waiting for you to come along. In France and Italy the police can even use your toll ticket as proof of speeding. The time of issue is printed on the ticket, so if you exit the motorway after 60 minutes, having covered 200km (120 miles), it doesn't take much to work out what you've been up to.

You may use a radar detector in Britain, where they occupy a legal grey area, though this is likely to change in the future. But they're illegal in most other countries, where they're seen for what they are: a means of breaking the law and trying to get away with it. Get caught using one, and you risk a big fine and having both detector and bike confiscated.

Finally, there are minimum speed limits on some motorways as well – it's 80kph (50mph) in France in good weather. This is worth bearing in mind if you really want to pootle, or are touring two-up on a 125.

Always obey speed limits, and even if there isn't an obvious deterrent like this one, law enforcement may be closer than you think

Blood/alcohol limits are often tighter abroad than they are in the UK, and the penalties just as severe. Golden rule on drinking and riding? Don't do it

Drink driving

There's a simple commonsense rule about drinking and riding while abroad, and it's the same one that applies in the UK – don't do it. It's particularly important for UK bikers to remember this, as our blood alcohol limit (80mg/100ml) is quite lax by international standards. The French limit is now 50mg/100ml and in Sweden it's just 20mg.

So even if you think you can safely down the odd pint in Britain before climbing back on the bike, you almost certainly can't in other countries. Some have a zero-tolerance drink-driving policy anyway, especially in Eastern Europe. In Hungary and the Czech Republic you aren't allowed to drink any alcohol whatsoever before riding.

Other countries impose tougher limits on younger riders and drivers. New Zealand has a lower 20mg limit for the under 20s, while in Australia it's 30mg for anyone under 25. The US's limit is 80mg, but with a legal drinking age of 21 anyone younger than that can't have a beer at all, even if they're the pillion.

Police all over the world are as tough on drink-driving as they are on speeding, if not more so, with a hefty fine being the least you can expect. Imprisonment is a possibility as well. Beware of drinking wine with lunch at a French roadside eatery – even with the food, it can make you drowsy on a hot afternoon, and will certainly impair concentration. Unfamiliar bottled beers can be stronger than the pint of bitter in your local back home too. Save that drink for the evening.

RULES AND REGULATIONS

Helmets

Helmets save lives, but, if you really insist, there are places where you are not legally obliged to wear one. However, there aren't many of them left. Judging by the number of bare heads in Greece you'd think there was no helmet law there, but there is. Italy has now made helmets compulsory on 50cc scooters as well as motorcycles. In Europe, the helmet you use has to comply with EU legislation.

Even in places where riding helmetless is legal, it may still invalidate your insurance, so it just isn't worth the risk, however tempting it may be. Some US states haven't made helmets compulsory (they're in the minority) though even these will insist on a lid for younger riders. So when ageing Harley riders speak of being 'in the wind', they're talking about what's left of their hair.

Florida, Texas and Louisiana are OK with helmetless riders, so long as they have medical insurance of at least $10,000. Most US states, even where helmets aren't compulsory, do insist on some form of eye protection, or else a screen of a minimum height.

The type of helmet you wear is really down to personal preference. Open-face helmets are great for short rides in sunshine, though they offer little face protection and are tiring over long distances, plus miserable when it rains. Full-face lids give the ultimate protection, though they can get a little claustrophobic in hot climates. The flip-up type is a good compromise, offering the best of both worlds, though they're heavier. Whatever type of helmet you use, comfort is vital if you're heading off abroad. If you're not used to high mileage, do some long day-rides at home first, to check your helmet stays comfortable over time. Always remove it at every stop, even if you're just filling up with fuel – ruffle that hair and let your scalp breathe.

It has to be said, riding without a helmet on a sunny day is wonderful, but not half so wonderful as keeping hold of all your faculties for the rest of your life.

Leave the lids
Carry a cable lock and fix your helmets to the bike. It's awful trudging around loaded up with kit, and helmets are one of the biggest chores. If it's likely to rain, cover them with a plastic bag – there's nothing worse than putting on a damp helmet.

Flip-up helmets are an excellent compromise between the fresh air of an open-face helmet and the protection of a full-face

Pillions need the same protection as riders, and the jeans and trainers worn by these two aren't recommended. Smart jackets, though

Pillions

Pillion passengers don't have to worry too much about legislation. Some countries impose a minimum age, which generally only applies to children under ten or so – in Britain, the rule is that a passenger's feet must reach the footrests. But other than wearing a helmet, the pillion has few legal obligations. One interesting exception in recent years was the Daytona Beach Bike Week in Florida, where the police decided to crack down on exuberantly 'in the wind' pillions by stipulating exactly how much bare flesh they were allowed to exhibit.

Even if the law is silent on the subject, a pillion should clearly have exactly the same protective gear as the rider – jacket, trousers, boots and gloves – as they're just as vulnerable in a crash. Pillions are not like car passengers: how they react affects the bike's handling, and they're just as much part of the machine as the rider is. So they need to stay alert and aware of what's going on around them, and shouldn't be tempted to drink at lunchtime any more than the rider. By the same token, pillion tiredness necessitates a stop to refresh, and the rider shouldn't press on regardless if his/her passenger is desperate to stop. Two hours is a guideline maximum for most of us, though some people will have a lower comfort threshold than this, some a higher one.

RULES AND REGULATIONS

Daytime lights

Daytime headlights are not compulsory in Britain, though most riders now use them, and on most modern bikes the headlight is wired to be permanently on with the ignition. Most European countries do expect you to keep the light burning all day, as do all US states, though a few of these exempt pre-1977 or (in one case) pre-1956 bikes, as an allowance for ancient electrical systems. If you do ride with daytime lights, they must be on dip, and in Europe pre-'97 bikes with twin headlights are allowed to have only one light showing on dip. Post-'97 machines may have both burning on dip.

Whenever the question of compulsory daytime lights comes up, the arguments range back and forth as to whether they actually make any difference. Unless the law compels it, it's really down to personal preference.

Filtering

Most countries allow filtering (sometimes known as 'lane splitting'), the act of trickling past a line of stationary or slow moving traffic. Some recommend limits, such as the speed difference between your bike and the cars not exceeding 20kph (12mph), and the cars themselves should not exceed 40kph (25mph).

In Germany, the law only permits filtering between the two outer (leftmost) lanes, and if there's a crash then the bike is automatically held to blame unless it can be proved (by a witness or police report) that the vehicle being overtaken did not show due caution. If they fling a door open or change lanes without warning, it's their fault – otherwise the responsibility lies with you. The Netherlands has a similar ruling, except that they assume a 50/50 split of blame, unless reckless driving can be proven.

In developing countries it's more of a free-for-all, but the consequences of a crash are just as serious if not more so. Oddly, it's in the land of the free that filtering is banned outright. If you reach a traffic jam

Under pressure

Check your tyre pressures. The bike will be carrying more weight than usual. When setting them, take account of the pillion and any high speed riding. If heading off-tarmac, different rules apply: soft sand requires a major decrease in pressure to increase grip, and your bike will handle better in loose thick gravel with slightly higher pressures.

Riding in unfamiliar traffic can be a daunting experience – taking your time and going with the flow is the best plan

Filtering law varies across the globe, but what local riders are doing is a good guide. The rules for doing it safely don't change though

in the United States, you have to sit there along with all the cars.

Where you are permitted to filter, the rules for doing it safely are the same everywhere. Keep the speed differential between yourself and the cars low enough so that you can stop if need be; keep horn and brakes covered; watch for cars changing lanes without warning, especially when one lane starts moving faster than the others; and look ahead – dangerous situations rarely happen as a bolt from the blue, they develop over a few seconds.

Parking

Parking in an unfamiliar town in a strange country isn't the nightmare for motorcyclists that it can be for car drivers, but you still can't park just anywhere. Some regions are quite happy for bikes to park on the pavement as long as they don't get in the way of pedestrians. Others will allow two-wheelers to use car spaces, but in some places that will get you a ticket. In others still, they won't mind as long as you make efficient use of the space with two or three bikes.

The best advice when searching for a bike space in a foreign town or city is to look for other bikes. They won't necessarily be parked in the official bike space (if there is one) but it should be legal. There's also the advantage of safety in numbers: a group of bikes is safer from theft than a lone machine.

Customs and Excise

Booze cruises may not be as popular as they used to be, but the tradition of duty-free is very much alive and well. Cigarette and alcohol smuggling is still a major issue for Customs and Excise, and the penalties are serious, and can include confiscation of your vehicle. So you must stay within the legal limits (see right), and anything you do bring back must be for personal use or as a gift – you can't supply friends and relatives if they reimburse you.

On a motorcycle, of course, you're regarded with

World of biking
Sitting outside a Parisian café, I watched a French scooterist ride nonchalantly straight onto the pavement, stick his machine on its sidestand and walk off, almost without pausing for breath. No one batted an eyelid. You wouldn't get away with that in London.

less suspicion, simply because it's trickier to squeeze a mountain of contraband under the seat, so you're less likely to be pulled over than the plain white Transit in front of you. But don't count on it.

Police
British police, the old saying used to go in less cynical times, are wonderful. And by and large, from a motorcyclist's point of view, most of them still are. Many of us have been stopped, only to be talked to and have the error of our ways calmly pointed out, rather than having a ticket automatically slapped on.

British police appear to be able to use their discretion with road users, but that isn't the case in all other countries. In Australia for instance, the national stereotype might lead to you expect a band of truly laidback law enforcers, but Australian police are as hot on speeding as anyone else. In Germany and France too, the police are more inclined to use the letter of the law when dealing with traffic violations, so if you're stopped, a fine, or worse, is a distinct possibility.

Being stopped by police abroad can be an intimidating experience. Not only are they unfamiliar, with the likelihood of a language problem, but many officers carry firearms and wear shades, which adds to the bristling atmosphere. In America, the police are just as likely to come across an armed driver as an unarmed one, so they'll be cautious.

So if the following police car puts its blue lights on (in the US, they may shine a red light at you, and/or give a loudspeaker command), stay calm. Don't stop immediately, but slow down and wait until there's a safe place to pull over. When you do, switch the bike off, take your helmet off (or flip-up, if you've got one of those) and rest your hands in sight, on the tank. All of this will reassure them that you're not about to take off. In many countries the police will expect a high degree of respect. Be polite and co-operative, and they'll invariably respond helpfully.

The situation is confused in some countries where

Customs limits for the UK

3200	cigarettes
400	cigarillos
200	cigars
3kg	tobacco
10	litres of spirits
20	litres of fortified wine
90	litres of wine
110	litres of beer

Police abroad require respect and co-operation. Show that, and they should be helpful in return

Contact with the police in foreign countries can seem intimidating, but they're doing the same job as colleagues in the UK

there are different grades or types of police, not all of whom can deal with traffic. In Italy, for example, there are four separate forces, of which the Vigili Urbani (local police) and Carabinieri (national police) can stop and fine road users. Whatever their classification, all police should be treated in the same way.

In Third World countries, the police have the same basic job to do and the same guidelines apply, though you may occasionally be asked for money, especially at national borders. Never try to pre-empt this by offering a bribe, and if you think one is being asked for, respond with an attitude of polite incomprehension; the officer will usually lose patience and allow you to ride on.

On-the-spot fines

In Britain, there is no such thing as an on-the-spot fine – even parking tickets allow a period of grace for you to pay up. Not so in much of the rest of the world, where police are empowered to hand out an on-the-spot fine and expect immediate payment, whether you're a local or a visitor.

It might seem harsh, but it prevents drivers on holiday from leaving the country (and thus local police jurisdiction) before the fine is due. At the moment, there is no legal mechanism to enforce a penalty once a driver has returned to their own country. However, this may change in the EU in the future, as there are proposals for the mutual recognition of penalties. If and when that happens, a speeding fine incurred in France will show up on your UK licence, and will hit your insurance premium next time round.

RULES AND REGULATIONS

How much you pay depends on the seriousness of the offence, though it usually only applies to speeding and minor infringements. It might be the whole fine, or just a deposit, with the bill for the full amount waiting for you at home. French police can enforce an immediate fine of up to €375, and in Belgium it can be up to €2,500 for non-residents (Belgians pay less).

The police will rarely take credit cards, though a Eurocheque may be acceptable. If you don't have sufficient cash with you, they'll escort you to the nearest cashpoint to draw some out – American police can do this as well. In serious cases, such as drink-driving, you could have your licence confiscated; this still won't affect your driving record in the UK, but you have to find a way of getting your bike home. This is a more likely scenario if you already have penalty points on your licence. If you've committed an offence that would take you over the points limit in that country, confiscation of the licence may result. The police can also be empowered to impound your bike, something worth bearing in mind when haring down the autoroutes.

In theory, you can legally contest on-the-spot fines by paying a deposit. But given the bureaucratic hassle, and the possibility of having to make a return trip to appear in court, it simply isn't worthwhile. Better to grit your teeth and pay up.

Early crossings
Outside Europe, border crossings may need a great deal of time and patience. The ideal is to get there early in the morning, and expect to spend all day dealing with officialdom. You'll be fresh from a good night's sleep, so you'll be more alert, more patient and better able to cope with the delays.

71

On the spot tickets and fines can be a feature of riding abroad. In extreme cases, you may have your bike impounded

DOCUMENTS
& ACCESSORIES

Riding through Europe is deceptively easy these days – you can travel from one side of the EU to the other without ever being stopped at a customs post. But don't let this fool you. Even riding through mainland Europe, it's vital to have the correct documents and insurance on hand, in case the local police ask for them. And travel insurance never seems necessary until you need it. So get all your paperwork in order before you go – it's one of the secrets of a stress-free trip.

Getting the paperwork in order is essential, and simpler than it might seem at first glance

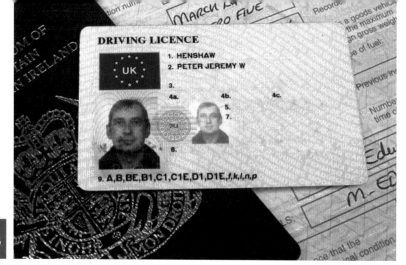

UK credit card sized driving licences are now to a standard EU design, and serve as a photo ID as well

Driving licence

Your valid driving licence must be kept with you at all times. Most countries insist that you always carry your licence (unlike the UK, where we're allowed seven days' grace to present it at the nearest police station) and it will be the first thing most police ask to see.

If you haven't got the latest credit-card-sized licence (which the DVLA began issuing in 1998) then it's well worth updating your old pink or green paper licence to that format. To a standard European design, it's accepted all over the EU. Better still, many countries require that you carry photo identification at all times, and the new licence satisfies that as well. If you haven't got one, you'll need to keep your passport with you as ID, and that's really better off in the security of the hotel safe.

To upgrade to a photocard licence, get application form D750 from a post office. It must be signed by a professional person (such as a doctor or teacher) and sent to the DVLA along with a passport photo and your passport or birth certificate. Processing takes around three weeks. There's a small fee (though not if you happen to be changing your address at the same time), but it's well worth it.

Even in this ID-conscious world, a tourist without valid identification isn't necessarily heading for jail, but keeping it with you all the time can save a great deal of hassle, especially when outside Europe. That's even more vital in troubled areas, where a police or military roadblock will demand (not ask) for ID – proving that you are who say you are is vital.

The UK driving licence allows you to ride abroad for a holiday or business trip, but if you're planning on staying for more than a few months, or settling down permanently, you may need to apply for a local licence. Check the regulations before you go.

Carry copies

Carry copies of your documents with you, and leave more copies with a person you trust at home – paperwork can be ruined by water, or stolen. As long as you can keep it safe, don't go out without your passport. If any original paperwork is lost/stolen, having copies will make the replacement process much quicker. Keep copies saved on an e-mail account as well.

DOCUMENTS & ACCESORIES

International Driving Permit

An International Driving Permit (IDP) is effectively an international driving licence, as it is recognised all over the world and proves that you have a valid licence at home. Just to underline the validity of this wonderful document, it is printed in ten languages, including Arabic, Russian and Chinese.

A long list of countries, from Afghanistan to Zimbabwe (see right), require that you carry an IDP, but this must always be in conjunction with your UK licence – it isn't sufficient on its own. In theory, this list should no longer include the latest (ex-Eastern Bloc) EU members, but it takes time for changes to reach the grassroots, so take one anyway. Even in Western Europe, you should have an IDP if you still have an old-style paper driving licence – Italian police no longer recognise the UK's old green licence.

Obtaining an IDP is simplicity itself. You simply send your driving licence and a passport photo, along with the application form and a small fee, to one of the motoring organisations, such as the AA or RAC. You don't have to be a member.

Countries which require an International Driving Permit (IDP):
Afghanistan
Albania
Algeria
Angola
Argentina
Benin
Bhutan
Brazil
Bulgaria
Cayman Isles
Central African Rep
Chad
CIS
Colombia
Comoros
Curacao
Czech Republic
Egypt
Equatorial Guinea
Guinea
Haiti
India
Indonesia
Iraq
Ivory Coast
Japan
Kampuchea
Kuwait
Leeward Islands
Macao
Nigeria
Pakistan
Philippines
Poland
Rwanda
Senegal
Slovenia
Somalia
South Korea
Surinam
Swaziland
Syria
Taiwan
United Arab Emirates
Vietnam
Zaire
Zimbabwe

The V5 registration document proves that you own the bike it refers to. If riding someone else's machine, you'll need documentation to prove that it is with their permission

Registration document

Alongside your driving licence, another vital piece of paper is the bike's registration document (V5). Few of us carry this around with us at home, but if the police stop you in a foreign country they'll want to see it, to confirm that you own the bike you're riding.

If you've only just bought the bike, and don't have the registration document yet (these things can take time…) then you can apply for a Temporary Certificate of Registration (V379). Pick up form V62 from a post office and send it to your local Vehicle Registration Office along with the bill of sale and proof of identity, plus the small fee.

If you've borrowed someone else's bike for your trip, you'll still need the registration document, plus written confirmation from the owner that you're entitled to ride it. This applies whether the legal owner is a leasing company, a hire company, or your best mate. In Portugal even this isn't enough, and you'll need a special certificate as well, which can be supplied by the motoring organisations.

Carnet

The carnet (Carnet de Passages en Douane, to give its full title) is a temporary import permit. It assures the government of the country you're visiting that you will take the bike out of the country within a limited time period, usually six to 12 months. That enables you to take the bike in without paying the duties and taxes that would normally be payable on a vehicle being permanently imported.

So the carnet is a vital piece of paper for serious travellers, allowing them to ride freely between countries all over the world. If you don't have a carnet, the alternative is to pay a large cash deposit, which you get back when you and the bike leave the country. But you won't need a carnet if you're riding into any European country, or anywhere in North, Central and South America – Ecuador used to be the exception, but it dropped its carnet requirement in 2004.

However, just about every other country in the world does insist on a carnet, and the regulations vary. For example, a common dream trip for many people is to fly to India, buy a new Royal Enfield Bullet and ride it home to Britain. But the Indian Government will not now issue carnets to non-nationals. The answer is to ride your new Bullet to Nepal (which will sell you a carnet) and head west from there. In Australia, a carnet for 12 months is available, and this can be extended, depending on the life of your visa. In New Zealand, the bike will have to undergo a safety inspection before it's allowed on the road. Some countries require a carnet if the bike is flown or shipped in, but not if you ride in overland.

One point that needs watching is that the carnet time limit may prove shorter than your own visa, which could lead to a nasty surprise (and a big fine) when you do come to leave. And of course, once you've crossed into your destination with the carnet, you must not sell the bike, which would be a serious offence.

Carnets are usually obtained from the relevant motoring organisation, which in Britain means the RAC.

MOT certificate
The quaintly named MOT (there hasn't been a 'Ministry of Transport' for years) is another essential if your bike is over three years old. If you're involved in an accident, it is evidence that the machine was in a roadworthy condition.

Vehicle excise duty
Otherwise known as VED (or better still, road tax), the only complication here is if you're planning to do a long trip and your tax disc is due to expire while overseas. Usually you can't apply for a new one more than two weeks in advance, but the DVLA will let you apply up to six weeks in advance, as long as you provide a letter explaining the reason. They will also send the disc to an overseas address.

Make a will
A morbid thought, but if you're heading off on a long, adventurous trip, do make sure your will is up to date. If the worst happens it's going to be hard enough as it is for the people you've left behind, but at least with a will properly set up they'll have a plan to follow. This can save endless unnecessary heartache.

Comprehensive insurance is vital to protect several thousand pounds worth of motorcycle. Peace of mind is priceless

EU members
Austria
Belgium
Denmark
Finland
France
Germany
Greece
Ireland
Italy
Luxembourg
Netherlands
Portugal
Spain
Sweden
UK
Cyprus
Czech Republic
Estonia
Hungary
Latvia
Lithuania
Malta
Poland
Slovenia
Slovakia

NB: the following
states are due to join
the EU in January 2007
Bulgaria
Romania

Bike insurance

Few things cause first-time tourists more anxiety than insurance. The good news is that your standard UK policy must by law provide third party cover in all EU countries, which now includes ex-Eastern Bloc nations like Poland, the Czech Republic and Latvia. The bad news is that third party is the minimum legal cover. If you have an accident, it will only cover the cost of vehicle damage and personal injury sustained by someone else. There's a much longer list of things it won't cover, including damage to your bike, any personal medical care, the cost of hiring a replacement bike and replacing any stolen items. So if you overcook it on a tricky hairpin and bend the forks, you're on your own, and it's the same if someone steals your tankbag.

The answer is to upgrade to fully comprehensive cover, which will take care of this. Some insurance companies (such as the AA) won't charge for this if you already have a fully comp policy, but others will. Either way, it's worth doing. Increasing your legal expenses cover is worth considering too, as making a claim in a foreign country, once you're back at home, can be costly and inconvenient to say the least.

One final thing: a comprehensive policy should also cover damage to the bike if it falls over on the ferry. This applies to recognised routes, but if it's an unusual one, or takes longer than 65 hours, then consult your insurance company to check.

Personal insurance

However comprehensive your bike insurance is, it won't necessarily cover all your medical costs if the worst happens, so it's always worth taking out a personal insurance policy as well (as long as you're not paying twice for the same cover).

Even if you don't have insurance, emergency medical care within the EU is covered by the European Health Insurance Card, which superseded the old E111 form on 1st January 2006. It can be applied for in post offices and travel agents, as well as on-line, and if it's valid, you will receive treatment. However, it should be treated like third party insurance – a good base, but not comprehensive.

Outside the EU, comprehensive personal insurance is an absolute must, and the Foreign Office recommends that travellers to the United States take out a minimum cover of $500,000.

Green Card

The Green Card is really the insurance equivalent of the International Driving Permit. Of itself, it doesn't provide insurance cover, but it is an internationally recognised symbol that proves you do have the minimum legal cover for the country being visited.

So although a Green Card is no longer compulsory within the EU, it's still worth having one, as it's much more widely recognised than the small print on an English language insurance certificate. Other countries (see right) insist on a Green Card anyway, and if you don't have one you'll have to purchase insurance at the border. An up-to-date list is available on the Association of British Insurers' website (www.abi.org.uk). Insurance companies don't charge for providing a Green Card, but brokers do.

Countries that require a Green Card

Albania
Andorra
Bosnia-Herzegovina
Bulgaria
Cyprus
Estonia
Iran
Israel
Latvia
Macedonia
Moldavia
Morocco
Poland
Romania
Tunisia
Turkey
Ukraine
Yugoslavia

79

Some countries still insist that you carry a Green Card – know before you go

It's unlikely, but if the bike does fail, then breakdown cover will save you a great deal of hassle, time and money. It's really worth having just for the peace of mind

Breakdown cover

Modern bikes don't break down, do they? If only it were true. A machine in perfect condition can still have a puncture or run out of fuel, or even suffer mechanical failure. The chances may be small, but think of the expense and hassle of being stranded in a country where you don't know the local term for 'ignition coil' or where the nearest dealer is. You might even have to pay to have the bike recovered all the way home, which is the time to take out a second mortgage.

The moral is to never leave home without some sort of breakdown cover. They vary from the cheap and cheerful (in which case be very clear about what you're buying) to the fully comprehensive. The latter can cover accommodation expenses and legal costs as well as finding spare parts and getting the bike repaired or taken home. Even if you never need cover like this, as the old saying goes, it's nice to know it's there.

Vignettes

We've already discussed motorway tolls, which in countries such as France and Italy are charged on a pay-as-you-go basis. Some Central European countries (including Austria, Switzerland, the Czech Republic and Slovakia) require you to buy a special tax disc instead, the vignette, which allows you to use motorways.

Vehicles driven abroad must show a national identifier. For bikes from Great Britain and Northern Ireland the identifier is GB (below); Alderney (GBA), Guernsey (GBZ), Jersey (GBJ) and the Isle of Man (GBM) have their own individual codes

These are widely available at border crossings, petrol stations and post offices, and can cover periods of ten days to a year or even longer, which vary from country to country. They're obviously not worth buying if you're intending to steer clear of motorways – which, given some of the marvellous roads in that part of Europe, is probably a good idea – but if you do ride on the motorway without a vignette, you risk being stopped by the police and fined.

See the section on individual countries for more information about vignettes.

DOCUMENTS & ACCESORIES

Essential accessories

Britain is the only EU member not to insist that all cars carry certain safety aids, such as a warning triangle, spare light bulbs, a first aid kit and a fire extinguisher. Lack of space precludes the first and last on a motorcycle, but spare bulbs and a basic first aid kit are a good idea anyway. Even if you don't feel confident using a first aid kit, someone else probably will.

Glasses

Here's a little-known piece of touring trivia: if you need to wear them, in Spain and Switzerland it's a legal requirement to carry a spare pair of spectacles or prescription sunglasses with you on the road. Get caught without them and you risk a fine. Luggage space allowing, a pair of prescription shades alongside your normal glasses are a good idea anyway.

GB sticker

The good old GB sticker is no longer compulsory if you have a Europlate, the number plate that includes the EU symbol with the letters GB beneath it. If you haven't got one of those, then you must have a GB sticker on any UK-registered bike ridden abroad.

Contingency fund
Money in reserve is a good idea, especially if you're doing a longer trip, to allow for things that may go wrong: breakdowns, closed borders or illness. Or for things that go right – the opportunity to head somewhere that wasn't in your original plan, for example. Being too tight on the budget can really take the shine off your trip.

81

If you don't have a Euro numberplate, you'll need a GB sticker

You'll need a headlight beam converter, to prevent your left-hand drive light dazzling oncoming drivers abroad

Headlight beam converter

UK-specification motorcycles dip their lights to the left, to avoid dazzling oncoming drivers and keep the side of the road well lit. Riding on the right, this is reversed, and your UK headlight will shine straight into the eyes of oncoming drivers. So it's compulsory to fit a headlight beam converter, a shaped sticker that blanks out the part of the beam that might dazzle. These are not expensive and are easy to fit. Of course, they should be removed as soon as you land back on British soil, as a beam converter will severely restrict your vision while riding on the left.

Fuel cans

The one drawback of motorcycles for serious travel is the relatively short distance they can cover on a tank-full of petrol. So if you're heading for remote areas, across Africa or parts of Asia, a spare fuel can is a very good idea. A steel jerrican full of fuel, securely mounted to the bike (and padlocked on, just in case someone takes a fancy to it), could be a lifesaver when crossing the Sahara, even though it is extremely heavy.

For riding anywhere else it simply isn't necessary to carry spare fuel, as even in the quieter parts of Europe and the United States you shouldn't have much trouble finding a filling station. Having said that, you need to take extra care on Sundays and national holidays. And if you don't know how far away the next filling station is, take the opportunity to fill-up whenever you can, even if you can only squeeze a few litres into the tank.

Have a good idea of what your bike's fuel range is, at the sort of speeds you'll be riding. It's especially useful to know how much you've got in reserve once the low-fuel light begins to flash, or, on those bikes which have one, when you turn the reserve tap on. The handbook should tell you how much fuel is on the reserve.

If you do run low, shift your riding style into economy mode, and you'll probably be amazed at how little fuel a motorcycle can use. The Yamaha TDM900 is a big, fast machine, which usually returns 40-50mpg ridden fairly hard. Low on fuel while touring Iceland, the author trundled a TDM along at a steady 55mph, two-up with luggage – the result was 75mpg!

Camping Card International

If you're camping, a Camping Card International (CCI) is highly recommended. It's a bit like the under-canvas equivalent of an International Driving Permit, recognised almost everywhere. A CCI will smooth your passage into campsites right across Europe, and brings other benefits, such as discounts at many sites and tourist attractions, not to mention third party insurance cover.

A CCI is actually compulsory if you want to stay at a campsite in Denmark or Portugal, while Norway and Sweden have compulsory cards of their own. CCIs can be obtained from one of the motoring organisations, or camping and caravanning clubs.

83

Don't skimp on camping
Go for the best quality sleeping mats, bags and tent you can afford. A good sleep is vital, so invest in a decent top-of-the-range kit. Check out the climate of where you're going. A three-season sleeping bag is good even in hot countries – at high altitude, or in the desert, even these can get chilly at night.

Camping gear means more to pack and carry, but gives you a wider choice of accommodation

HIRING
AND SHIPPING

Riding your own bike to some far-flung destination is all very well, but it adds hugely to the cost, and most of us simply don't have the time to take a six-month trip. The alternative is to take the train, plane or boat, and hire a bike once you get there.

This option is now easier than ever before, and bike hire is something of a boom industry in certain areas of the world. You can rent a Harley to ride Route 66 across the US, or hire a Honda VFR to explore the twisting, scenic roads of New Zealand. For the more adventurous, trail bikes can be hired to visit the remoter parts of South-East Asia, South Africa or India. Or perhaps you just want a small bike or scooter on which to explore local roads around your hotel. All of this is now possible, though there are, of course, pitfalls awaiting the unwary.

Hiring a scooter or motorcycle frees you from the ties of taxis, public transport and organised coach tours

The internet is a good place to start when researching bike hire, and all reputable hirers will have English language websites

How to hire

How to hire really depends on what sort of bike you're looking for. Renting a small machine or a scooter, to use locally at your destination, is usually done after you've arrived. There are plenty of hire outlets in the popular holiday destinations, especially in Greece, and your hotel or a tourist information desk will soon point you in the right direction.

The hire period can be anything from half a day to a week or more. Look out for special offer seven-day deals, which can sometimes work out cheaper than hiring for five days at the normal rate. Bikes do get booked up in the peak season, and at that time of year booking your bike should be one of your first priorities, even if you're not intending to collect it for a couple of days. At either end of the season, when demand is slack, it's often worth bargaining for a reduction or an extra day on the hire period.

If you want to hire a bigger bike, then it's best to spend some time researching on the web before you go. Typing 'motorcycle rental' and your destination into a search engine should bring up several alternatives. Companies renting out big bikes are fewer in number though, so their location may determine where you go in the first place.

Glean as much information as you can from the website, such as the age and type of bike available, exactly what is included (or not) and the small print. Phone or e-mail if you have any questions, and don't commit yourself until you're satisfied. Because customers will be riding longer distances, many of these companies will be happy to suggest scenic routes. It helps if you can give them an idea of the sort of riding you want to do – twisty mountain roads, beach cruising or rolling hills. Some will also work out a whole itinerary for you in advance, and even book the accommodation.

If you don't wish to ride on your own, there are plenty of companies which include bike hire as part of a guided tour, in which the motorcycle-mounted guide will lead a group of bikes over a pre-planned

HIRING AND SHIPPING

itinerary. You don't have to book these trips as a group – most are made up of like-minded individuals, so it's a great way of making new friends.

Your documents

You must have a full motorcycle licence in order to hire a bike, wherever it is in the world. This has always been the case with big machines, but things have now tightened up for the scooters as well. In Greece, probably the tourist-on-rented-scooter capital of Europe, the accident rate used to be horrendous, because young holidaymakers with little or no riding experience were permitted to rent; but you now have to have held a bike licence – valid for the machine you're renting – for at least a year. Helmets are compulsory as well now, even for mopeds.

As well as the licence, you should also have your International Driving Permit (IDP), just as if you were riding your own bike. As a rule, hiring a small scooter for a day is a more casual affair than taking charge of a Harley-Davidson for two weeks, but it's still just as well to have the IDP with you, in case anything goes wrong.

Learn to tyre change
Removing/replacing each wheel and tyre and repairing a puncture is an important skill if you're outside the remit of breakdown cover. If heading for remote areas, you might have to do it yourself, and it's better to cope with the learning curve in your garage than on a Moroccan plain.

Whatever you hire, you'll need all the right documentation. Before signing up, give the bike an inspection, especially the tyres

Hiring a big bike like this isn't a cheap option, so make sure you know what's included in the deal. Maybe a smaller, cheaper machine will do the job just as well?

Choosing the right bike

Once again, this depends on the sort of riding you want to do, though it may be that you've always had a dream of riding a Goldwing, or a Harley, and hiring is the best way to do it.

If you just want to potter around locally, seeking out quiet beaches or remote tavernas, then a 250cc bike or even a 125cc scooter will be perfectly adequate. Most experienced bikers will prefer the motorcycle – scooters are fun, but their smaller wheels give less stable handling, especially on gravel roads. Also, if you're two-up, 250cc is a minimum unless you really are only riding a few miles from base.

As for the big bikes, if you're itching to ride a sports bike like a Yamaha R1 or a Suzuki GSX-R then you'll probably be disappointed. These very rarely come up for hire, for the good reason that their high performance can get less experienced riders into trouble very quickly. The best way to experience one of these bikes is to stay in the UK and have a track day, which includes the bike hire and on-track tuition and caters for sports bike novices as well as more experienced riders.

Most hire companies concentrate on the big tourers – BMWs, Goldwings, Harleys and Pan Europeans –

You can even hire classic bikes in India (the ubiquitous Bullet) and parts of Europe now – perfect for lower mileage, lower speed tours as well as large 'naked' bikes like the Suzuki Bandit 1200 and sports tourers such as the Honda VFR. Any of these will happily carry two people plus their luggage many miles each day, in reasonable comfort. But it's still worth bearing in mind the sort of roads you'll be travelling. A full-dress Harley, if you're not used to the weight, can be quite a handful on hairpin-heavy mountain roads, though it's perfect for cruising the Florida Keys.

Big bikes are undeniably expensive to hire, and if you're on a budget many companies also offer smaller machines such as the Yamaha Diversion 600 or BMW F650. As long as you restrict your daily mileage a little, these bikes will still take two people a long way in a day. And the money saved might give you a few extra days' holiday.

Luggage

Most hire bikes come with some sort of luggage, whether hard cases or soft panniers. It's essential that you check this before arriving, or you might be charged an unexpected extra when you collect the bike. If the bike doesn't include luggage, it's best to bring your own soft panniers/tankbag as hand luggage, and strap it on when you arrive.

Waterproof packing
Hard luggage should be waterproof, but don't count on it, and soft luggage almost certainly won't be, so pack everything in clear plastic bags (so that you can see what it is). Use square or oblong plastic tubs for fragile items. The extra layer also helps with friction rub when you're riding off-road.

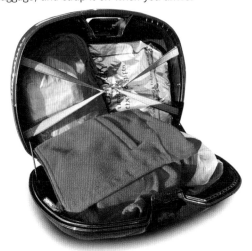

Check in the small print that the hire bike comes with luggage, though it should do

You might be riding a hire bike, but there's no substitute for your own helmet and bike kit, which fits you and is a known quantity. Choose what you wear according to the climate

Clothing and helmet

As with luggage, most hire firms will include a helmet as part of the package. However, with smaller bikes and scooters this is likely to be an ageing open-face lid – tempting in a hot climate, but it's a far better idea to take your own helmet, which fits you and (hopefully) is of good quality. Ignore the fact that very few locals are wearing helmets – it doesn't mean the law allows it, and even if it does (few places do these days) it's never a good idea.

It's also tempting, especially when riding a small bike locally in sunny climes, to not bother with biking gear. Sadly, Southern European hospitals have lots of experience dealing with badly injured tourists who were happily riding in shorts and T-shirt (or even a bikini) until they came off.

That doesn't mean you have to wear full leathers, but a denim jacket, decent leather gloves and padded jeans will give good protection in low-speed accidents. Put your shorts in the topbox – you can slip them on when you get to the beach.

Companies hiring big bikes may offer clothing hire as well, though it's worth checking they have your sizes before leaving home. Better still, take your own gear. As with the helmet, it fits properly and is a known quantity. Just take into account the climate you'll be riding in.

Age limits

Young riders are far more likely to be involved in an accident than older ones. Hire firms know this, and charge accordingly. As a 19-year-old with a full licence, you shouldn't have much trouble hiring a scooter or small motorcycle, but there's likely to be an insurance surcharge. But companies hiring out bigger machines are very unlikely to contemplate anyone under 25 – some stipulate a minimum age of 30. This is usually a requirement passed on by their own insurance company, rather than simple discrimination against the young.

HIRING AND SHIPPING

Crossing borders

If you intend to ride your rented bike into a different country, it's always worth checking this with the hire firm beforehand. US companies are usually OK about you taking the hired Harley into Canada, but are less relaxed if you're aiming to ride south into Mexico.

In the EU, flitting between EU member states shouldn't be a problem at all, though some companies may put restrictions on travelling into Eastern Europe, even those states which are now part of the EU.

If you are intending to cross borders (especially outside the EU) you'll need to carry all the relevant paperwork with you, to prove that you're entitled to be riding a bike that's registered under someone else's name.

Border crossings may be complicated if you are on a hired bike, though it shouldn't be a problem within the EU – once again, check the small print

Even if you hire an off-road bike, the insurance won't necessarily cover it for riding off-tarmac, or on gravel roads

Insurance

You might expect that hiring a bike would include comprehensive insurance. After all, surely it's in the hire firm's interest to cover their own bike? Unfortunately, things aren't that simple, and once again you need to check the small print before riding off. If the basic hire price only includes third party or liability insurance, this will only cover damage to other vehicles, and injury to other people. The cost of damage to the hire bike, or injury to yourself or your passenger, will be entirely down to you.

If this is the case, many hire companies will offer a means of upgrading the insurance for an extra fee. The first thing to look for is Collision Damage Waiver (CDW), which covers damage to the bike. This is well worth having, as even quite minor spills can be very expensive on a big touring bike with an expanse of shiny bodywork. You must also have Theft Protection (TP) to prevent your holiday coming to a premature and colossally expensive end. Of course, all the commonsense rules about security (see page 112) apply just as much to a hire bike as your own machine.

Even after taking out these extra policies, there's almost certain to be an excess. If the excess is £500, you will pay for the first £500 of any repairs. Again, you may be able to pay extra for an Excess Reduction (ER) fee, which will reduce the excess. But even if the excess is zero, some parts such as tyres may not be covered.

Whatever the insurance policy, it may not cover use of the bike on gravel roads – this may even apply to off-road style bikes, so check with the hire firm. It shouldn't be a problem when hiring a trail bike in South-East Asia, where it will be difficult to avoid dirt roads in the more remote parts, but it's still worth checking.

Legal insurance is highly recommended in the litigious United States, and will cover you against third parties suing you for damages. This is called Supplementary Liability Insurance (SLI) or Extended Protection (EP), and $1m of cover is a good figure to have. Also check whether the hire package includes breakdown cover. If not, the entire costs of any breakdown, including returning the bike whence it came, could be down to you.

All of this sounds essential, but it's also worth checking your own personal insurance, to avoid paying for the same thing twice. It's unlikely your UK motorcycle policy will offer much cover, but travel insurance may well include legal cover, and theft of personal possessions. Insurance, it has to be said, is not a riveting subject, but knowing you're properly covered will allow you to spend a stress-free time on the bike.

Tired? Ill? Stop!
If you have an objective, the temptation is to push on, even if you're tired or not feeling 100 per cent. Either of these situations can mean that you never get there at all, and you may badly hurt someone else along the way.

Hiring a Harley is a great way to tour North America, and the package should include comprehensive insurance cover

94 *Tyres are an excellent indicator of how well a hire bike has been maintained*

Collecting the bike

Collecting a rental bike is just like buying second-hand. You're entrusting your life to this machine, so you need to have a good look over it to check that all is in order. If you can, do this before signing the agreement, though most big-bike hire firms are reputable and it's highly unlikely that any would try to palm you off with a dangerous machine.

All the same, look past the shiny paintwork and polished chrome to the tyres – an excellent indicator of how well the bike is being looked after. Even if they're partly worn, do they have enough life to last your entire trip? The last thing you want to do is spend a day of your holiday waiting for new tyres to be sourced and fitted. Worn footrests and handgrips are a good indication of how many miles the bike has covered (whatever the mileometer may say). As for the bodywork, make a note of any existing damage and point it out, which will save you being charged for it later on.

When you finally come to ride away, take it easy for the first few miles, and get to know what is, after all, an unfamiliar bike. How do the brakes feel, how does it handle, does the engine sound sweet? If you're really unhappy about something, take the bike back as soon as possible. But just to reiterate, this is most unlikely with any reputable hire company.

Collecting a small bike or scooter needs care too. With lower prices and a higher turnover of riders, the hire company may be tempted to skimp on maintenance, and we've all heard the horror stories about death-trap scooters for rent to gullible tourists. Just take all the same precautions as you would with a big bike, and if you're not happy with the way the machine rides, take it back.

HIRING AND SHIPPING

Returning the bike

Don't worry too much about returning the bike bang on time. Most rental companies who hire by the day will give you an hour or so's grace before charging for an extra day. It's certainly not worth riding back at breakneck speed to meet the deadline.

Some companies will want the bike returned with a full tank of fuel (otherwise they'll fill it themselves and probably charge you at a less than generous rate). Others include the first tank in the hire charge, so the emptier the tank when you return, the cheaper your holiday – it's not worth risking running out three miles from the hire shop, though, especially if you have a plane to catch.

The hire company will give the bike a good look over to check you haven't damaged anything, and it's best if they do that before you've left. They'll usually have your credit card details already, and when you get home you might find you've been charged for damage that you weren't responsible for.

Some of the firms that hire out big bikes will also offer an airport transfer service, either as part of the package or as an extra. Depending on where they're located, this could save a lot of hassle, though a local bus is bound to be cheaper.

Keep a diary
It's so easy to forget valuable moments when every day is full of surprises, so keep a daily diary. Who knows, you might have enough adventures to fill a book!

95

All the precautions about picking up, checking over and returning a motorcycle apply to a scooter as well

96

Shipping your own bike abroad is worthwhile if you're planning a longer trip, and gives you a familiar companion when you get there

Shipping

Some riders simply don't want to hire a bike, but would rather ship their own out to their destination. This gives you the advantage of riding a machine that you know, which is quite handy on unfamiliar roads in unfamiliar conditions. Better still, you probably won't worry quite so much about the odd scratch, whereas a hire bike (especially an expensive one) can make you paranoid about insurance excess. And although shipping your own bike across the world will never be cheap, it can work out less expensive than hiring if you're planning on a trip of a month or more.

Shipping overland is a possibility within Europe, and the first step is to search for a local haulier in the Yellow Pages. Find one that offers regular runs to your intended destination, as this will be cheaper than one that has to make a special journey. The bike should ideally be crated (your local dealer may be able to help here), with all vulnerable parts such as levers and indicators wrapped in plenty of foam or bubble wrap.

Crating a bike (there are two here!) for shipping needs care, to keep dimensions to a minimum and everything secure

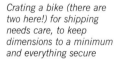

An alternative, if you don't fancy placing your bike at the mercy of a haulier, is to use the Motorail service. This runs from Calais down to the south of France, with connections to other parts of Europe. You will have to accompany the bike, but on a sleeper service it can mean waking up in Southern Europe with your bike ready and waiting. It's quicker than riding down, and a lot more relaxing.

For longer distance shipping, say to North America, to Africa or Australia, the choice is between sea freight and air freight. Opinions differ as to whether it's really cheaper by sea, but it usually is, though of course it does take longer than air freight. It can take nine days for a bike to cross the Atlantic westwards (and three weeks coming back) but only two days to fly. If going by sea, the choice is between uncrated and crated. Uncrated is quicker and more straightforward, though of course the bike is more vulnerable to damage. A crated machine is more secure, and the agent can collect/deliver the bike, and even crate it for you, but the whole process takes longer.

Either way, preparation is limited to a good clean (there should be no mud or squashed insects getting a free ride), the luggage should be empty, and the fuel tank nearly so. After sailing you'll be sent the Bill of Lading. This proves you've paid for the shipment and enables you to collect the bike at the other end. Taking delivery at the docks can take some time – allow at least half a day – depending on where you are in the world.

One tip that really cuts the cost of sea freighting is to pool resources with other riders and hire a whole or half container, which is worth doing if ten or more bikes are being shipped together. This can cut the cost of shipping by up to 50 per cent; it's a perfect solution for clubs, and can make shipping your machine to the other side of the world relatively affordable.

But air freight remains the quickest, if not the cheapest, means of shipping. The first step is to contact the major airline cargo divisions, who can quote you a price, given the bike's weight and dimensions. There is more bike preparation involved than with sea freight – the battery must be disconnected or even removed, and you may be required to drain all petrol and oil as well. The bike will also have to be X-rayed before it goes on board (and it can be a problem for larger machines to physically fit through the X-ray equipment). As with sea freight, you do need to check whether transit insurance is included. But air freight doesn't have to be long distance – it's a favourite for bikers making the hop between Central and South America.

97

Carry some straps
Mini ratchet straps come in handy all the time. They work as tie-downs on the ferry, as washing lines, as spare guy lines on stormy nights and of course, those vital souvenirs have to be strapped on somehow. Cable ties are cheap, light and easily carried, and they can prove more useful than you'd ever think possible.

EXTREME
CONDITIONS

Motorcycling in Britain is easy. It might not seem like it on a dark, dank winter's morning, but we have a mild, benign climate offering none of the extremes experienced elsewhere in the world. All of our public roads, apart from a tiny minority, are well surfaced.

But you don't have to travel far to find rather more challenging riding conditions. Travel to the Alps, or even the Highlands of Scotland, and you'll find more snow than southern England has seen for many years. Further afield the roads deteriorate into dirt, gravel and mud. Many of us, on tour in the summer on tarmac roads, will never encounter conditions like this, but some will, and this chapter describes how to survive rocky roads and poor weather.

99

You're unlikely to encounter conditions like this, unless a longer trip takes you into winter, but extreme roads can be challenging in summertime too

Snow

Believe it or not, there are enthusiasts out there who
deliberately take their bike out into the snow. Not a
quick dash and a bit of fun on a trail bike, but proper
long-distance touring. There are even winter events to
cater for them, such as the Dragon Rally in Wales
and the Elephant in Germany, held every year.

If you want to tackle an event like that, you'll need
to make particular preparations. Heated clothing and
heated grips are the only sure way to keep warm
over a long ride in freezing conditions, and there is
plenty of choice. Heated grips are fairly simple to
wire into the bike, while clothing connects directly to
the battery. Do beware that this will drain a lot of
electrical power, especially if your pillion is centrally
heated too, so it's best to switch off the heat 10-15
minutes before you stop for the night, to give the
battery a chance to recharge properly.

Serious snow-bound tourists fit studs to their tyres
when they reach the white stuff (or carry a spare set
of tyres, ready studded). These dramatically improve
your grip in snow and ice, but they're no guarantee
that you won't fall off.

However, most of us won't encounter snow while
on holiday, unless it's unplanned.

*Warning of the risk of ice
on the road, this sign is
widely used throughout
Europe, and gives a
useful indication of where
extra care may be needed
in cold weather*

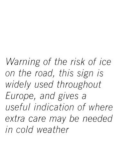

EXTREME CONDITIONS

Rain and floods

One thing we are familiar with in Britain is rain and (increasingly, as climate change takes hold) floods. But these rarely arrive without warning, whereas in some hot, dry countries the opposite is the case.

Inadequate drains, and less vegetation to soak up the rain, can lead to roads running knee-deep in water very quickly. Bikes are better able to deal with moderate floods than cars, because their air intakes are usually higher, and you don't need to worry about water spoiling the carpets. But you still shouldn't attempt to ride through a flood until you're sure how deep it is, either by wading through or watching someone else have a go.

If you're convinced the water level is lower than your air intake, then ride through steadily in first or second gear. Keep up the revs (which will prevent the engine stalling if the tailpipe is under water) by slipping the clutch. Also, try to keep to the crown of the road, where the water should be shallower. Once out the other side, apply the brakes a few times to dry them out. With any luck you'll have emerged with no more than wet feet. With decent boots, you shouldn't even have those.

Experienced riders will know to slow down and leave more space around the bike when travelling on wet roads. In hot countries, the rain may have come after a prolonged dry spell, during which a film of oil and rubber has accumulated on the tarmac. Mixed with water this becomes a skating rink, so take care.

Inadequate run-off may allow water to collect in large puddles, which can be scary to hit at speed. If you do, and the front end goes light as it loses contact with the road, don't brake. Just roll off the power gently and the bike will stabilise as it slows and the front tyre regains its grip. Watch out for dips in the road where water can accumulate, especially at night, when you may not see the water until you hit it.

Keep warm and watered

Dehydration and hypothermia can creep up on you. Both will badly impair your reactions, so even if you're tempted to just ride though it and get to your destination, make enough time to stop and warm up or have a swig of water.

101

Flooded roads aren't always this well signed, and standing water can be a serious hazard at night

You don't need a trail bike and knobbly tyres to ride a good gravel road like this, but the technique still needs care

Gravel roads

In Britain, where even the most minor single-track roads are smothered in tarmac, we very rarely ride on gravel or dirt – a car park is the closest some bikers get to riding off-road. It is possible to traverse South America and Asia (let alone Europe and North America) and rarely if ever leave tarmac. However, if you ride through Africa, tarmac is in the minority, and in South Africa and Australia even quite major roads may be left with a gravel surface, albeit a nicely graded and well maintained one. Iceland is also famous for its gravel highways.

The good news is that there is no mystique about riding on gravel, and well-maintained gravel roads can easily be ridden on a normal road bike without knobbly tyres. But you do need to take a lot more care than when riding on tarmac – you may be able to skim along in a straight line at tarmac speeds on a deceptively smooth surface, but your cornering and stopping powers will be drastically reduced. Slam the brakes on, the wheels will lock up instantly, and you'll learn all about gravel rash at first hand.

To avoid this, use the same techniques as when riding on any treacherous surface. Above all, ride smoothly, feeding in the power gradually, and ideally don't use the brakes at all. In deep gravel, keep the power on, which should lighten the front end a little and prevent it from digging in. If you have to, brake smoothly and gently. Several bikes are now equipped with ABS (anti-lock brakes) which helps, but don't rely on these to get you out of trouble.

Many gravel roads are hardly maintained at all, which allows corrugations to build up. These are a

EXTREME CONDITIONS

jarring succession of undulations which can persist for 20 minutes of riding, though you can sometimes avoid them by searching for smoother sections at the side or centre of the road. Also watch out for seasonal water courses in dips, which can leave a deposit of thick gravel and even boulders.

If you're heading for roads like these, and you have little or no off-road experience, then an off-road riding course is highly recommended. One-day courses are available in several parts of Britain, and in that short time they'll teach you a lot about controlling a bike off-tarmac, as well as do wonders for your confidence. All these courses include the use of a trail bike.

Mud and rivers

We think we know a thing or two about mud in Britain, but it's nothing compared to the quagmires you'll encounter on the tracks heading through Central African jungles. These are near impassable on a touring bike, and most travellers riding through here use proper trail bikes with knobbly tyres. Letting a little air out of the tyres will help traction, but often the only technique is to paddle through at a walking pace. This is especially true of deep ruts, which are sometimes the only place where it's possible to ride.

If you really want to explore remote areas of the world, sooner or later you'll have to cross a river without the benefit of a bridge or a boat. The same advice applies as when tackling flooded tarmac. Be absolutely sure of the depth first, by wading through, which in the case of a river will give you a chance to check the surface. If it seems rideable, then keep the revs high in first or second gear and ride through steadily. Resist splashing, which can wet the electrics – a spray of WD40 around the plug cap and other ignition parts will help before you go in. Above all, don't go in deeper than your air intake height: if the engine takes in water, it will 'hydraulic', bending the crankshaft or con-rod as the piston tries to compress water (which won't).

Early start, early stop 103

An early start gives you the whole day to play with, with more time to explore in daylight when you reach your destination. Early arrival means that you'll have the pick of the hotels and camping spots too. It's never worth riding a strange land at night. Your senses aren't as sharp, and there's too much that you won't see until the last minute.

If in any doubt, check the depth of any river or flood before riding in, and find the easiest (least rocky) way through

No doubts about the route here, but navigation in remote areas can be a nightmare, with tempting tracks heading off in all directions

In the desert

Riding across deserts is more popular than ever before, thanks to a new generation of adventuresome bikers, and the availability of the right bikes for the job. Desert travel is challenging in a different way to other riding, as making certain mistakes may cost you your life.

Riding through sand requires its own technique. It's fine when consistently firm, but it very rarely is, and you need to be on the watch for patches of soft sand that will suck your momentum away until you come to a halt, back wheel spinning uselessly as it digs the bike into a hole. To avoid this, drop the tyre pressures significantly, to as little as 5psi. This increases the tyre 'footprint' and greatly increases traction. However, the tyre will get hotter due to internal friction, and the pressure should be returned to normal as soon as you reach firm ground. The other essential is to keep up momentum – don't be afraid to accelerate through soft sand. The bike will weave around, but you should get through: trying to slow down will actually make the bike less stable. And don't use the brakes unless you really have to.

If the bike does get bogged down, it may be possible to extricate it by hopping off and walking it out using a combination of engine and muscle power, then hopping on again once you reach firm ground. If that doesn't work, and the bike digs itself in, lie it on its side and kick sand back into the hole made by the spinning rear wheel, before using the walk-out technique.

If the worst happens and the bike breaks down or runs out of fuel, don't try and walk to safety unless you're on a really remote piste (track) – leaving the bike really is a last resort, when all else fails. As long as the piste is reasonably well used, another vehicle should come along eventually. It's important to arrange some sort of protection from the sun, using the bike as a prop, and you should also take stock of food and water supplies. There have been cases where stranded bikers have attracted the attention of a distant passing vehicle by setting fire to a tyre or even the seat. That's definitely in the last resort category, though.

Navigation

Navigation in remote desert or mountainous areas, with non-existent road signs, seems daunting. But with common sense, a compass and a good map, it need not be. You need to make use of landmarks – a fork in the road, or a hill – and also of the bike's tripmeter, to be sure of how far you've travelled and thus know where you are. Armed with that knowledge, putting a mistake right shouldn't be too difficult, even if you've strayed far from where you should be.

It might be tempting to just keep following an apparently well-used track without reference to landmarks or distance travelled, but this can easily get you lost. Such desert tracks may lead nowhere at all. Frequent stops to check the map, compass and any landmarks are essential. You'll still make swifter progress than if you got lost and had to backtrack.

In theory, GPS systems (see page 28) offer a high tech answer to all of this, being able to pinpoint your position within a few metres without reference to any sort of landmark. Used to supplement a good map and your own common sense, they're a real asset.

(see page 28)

Take a hike
When you stop for a rest, as well as sitting down walk around for a few minutes. This gets your muscles working, and your heart and lungs pumping, and can be quite refreshing. Your body will deal with longer rides better if you take exercise during the day.

Sand can look deceptively smooth, but can also hide soft patches that will slow you faster than the brakes – use momentum to get through them

Riding far from the nearest tarmac gives a sense of adventure and achievement

The Third World

Riding in the Third World can be extremely dangerous, and more so in urban areas than out in the sticks. Riding across London at rush hour may sometimes seem like taking your life into your hands, but it's tame compared to traffic conditions in many parts of Africa and Asia.

In Europe, we've had a good hundred years to get used to motor vehicles, and only in the last 30 years have road safety measures really begun to work. But in the Third World vehicle ownership has only begun rising quite recently, with little chance for familiarity with vehicle speeds, or an awareness of road safety, to develop.

India is often quoted as an example of high crash rates, a terrible death toll and fatalistic drivers. On a busy road, it's not unusual to see vehicles three abreast (car overtaking truck overtaking bus), and the usual rule of the road is that size matters. Motorcycles come somewhere near the bottom of the pecking order, between bicycles and cars.

So expect drivers to do the exact opposite of what you'd expect: stopping in the middle of the road for no apparent reason; doing a U-turn across several lines of traffic without warning; and not giving way where they clearly should. In these conditions, your horn is a vital asset, not as a post-event blast of frustration, but in advance, to warn drivers that you're there.

All the usual advanced riding techniques, such as anticipation, and creating as much space as possible around your bike, will stand you in good stead here. And remember that drivers who cut you up are not necessarily being deliberately aggressive – it's just the way things are done.

EXTREME CONDITIONS

Alpine riding

Even if you steer clear of their challenging winter rides, the Alps provide challenge enough in perfect conditions. Britain has few mountains, and few of our classified roads climb above 2,000ft (600m), but in France the highest mountain pass (the Col de Restefond) peaks at nearly 9,000ft (2,680m).

For motorcyclists, these heights provide some spectacular roads. There's nothing to compare with starting off in an Alpine valley and snaking your way up a mountainside, through thick pine forest which gradually gives way to sparser vegetation until you emerge into the bleak and rocky world above the snowline. Then you crest the pass, to be rewarded with a terrific view over the other side. There's often a café at the top of the pass serving excellent coffee as well. Riding roads like this can be challenging as well as exhilarating, though you need to have a head for heights: you may be riding just a couple of feet away from a precipice, with only a piece of Armco between you and oblivion.

Hairpin bends need concentration, especially on a big bike laden down with passenger and luggage. Going up, get all your braking done before entering

Take medication
If you need specialist medication, take enough to last the trip. And crucially, have a doctor's certificate that confirms why you need it. Some of us have no choice but to travel with medication in quantity, and this can make police stops or border crossings more stressful than they need to be. An official and translated certificate will usually do the trick.

107

More proof that a modest bike will cope with a few off-road miles – Enfield Bullets in Spain

If you like bends, you'll love the Alps, with their almost endless selection of mostly well surfaced hairpins

the bend, then use engine power to smoothly drive the bike through. Going down, make full use of the gears to maximise engine braking and if necessary use the rear brake gently in the corner, to steady the bike. Locals who know the road will often want to get past, so pull over to make room, which they'll appreciate. Also watch for coaches coming the other way, especially on sharp bends, where they may have to swing on to your side of the road to get round.

Minor roads in the Alps are often single-track, with plenty of blind bends. There's little traffic on these routes, but there could always be a car, or livestock, around the next corner. If you meet something after a few miles of deserted tarmac, don't forget you should pull over to the right – it's all too easy to give in to the UK rider impulse to keep left. On hilly single-track roads, the general rule is for the vehicle going down to give way to the one coming up, and this is often backed up by law. In Austria, the vehicle that finds it easiest to stop has to do so. When you're trying to balance a heavy bike on a steep hill with an awkward camber, it's clearly easier for the oncoming car to stop than it is for you, but don't count on them recognising this.

These sorts of roads will put a lot of strain on your bike. Big tourers should shrug the climbs off with no trouble, but on any bike you still need to watch for signs of overheating (especially if you get stuck behind a slow moving coach on a hot day). If the temperature gauge is close to the red zone (or with an air-cooled engine, if the motor starts 'pinking') just stop and let it cool down. Winding down the other side, you need to keep an eye on the brakes, especially if the pads are worn. This isn't quite so

Always give way to post office vehicles in Switzerland on roads marked with this blue rectangle showing a yellow horn. Some Swiss roads are one way, but at certain times of day only. Pay careful attention to the signs at each end of the road which advise when the priority changes

EXTREME CONDITIONS

critical as for cars, as motorcycles have excellent engine braking, which takes a lot of strain off the brakes.

The higher you go, the colder it gets, so climbing to high altitudes can bring unexpected changes in conditions. Even if it's a sunny, warm morning in the valley floor you set off from, the temperature can be freezing at the top of a pass, even in summer. So watch out for shadows cast on the road by trees and rocks, where there may still be ice lurking. If you do hit a patch of ice, the first sign will be a lightness at the front or back before the bike starts to move around. Do not brake, just gently roll off the power and let the bike recover as it reaches dry tarmac again.

Picture tips
Take photos in the morning and late afternoon if possible – the midday sun can make pictures looked washed out. If you can afford it, and have the space, try taking two cameras, a pocket-sized job to be with you always, and a larger more adaptable camera for zoom and filter shots.

Beware of other tourist traffic in scenic areas, especially coaches on tight mountain roads

IN AN
EMERGENCY

Breaking down, crashing or having someone steal your bike is far less likely to happen abroad than you might think. Most bikers will come home without having suffered any of these problems. But they can still happen, and are more difficult to deal with than they would be at home, with a foreign language and unfamiliar surroundings adding to the stress. This chapter looks at how to cope with emergencies. Just as important, it also advises you how to help prevent these things happening in the first place.

It's unlikely you will encounter a genuine emergency when riding abroad, but it's as well to be prepared

A decent alarm/immobiliser is a fine deterrent to thieves, but take care where you park, too

Security

Security is a big issue for motorcyclists – you can't lock things away out of sight on a bike as you can in a car, unless you have hard luggage. On the other hand, this does bring the discipline of always carrying everything valuable with you rather than leaving it vulnerable to the light-fingered.

But there's one thing you can't get away from. Abroad, a heavily-laden motorcycle with a British number plate is conspicuously on holiday, and to the professional thief that spells money, passports, credit cards and cameras. And of course, the bike itself is also vulnerable to theft, though factory-fitted features such as an immobiliser, and marked components that are difficult to resell, have greatly improved bike security in recent years. Many riders fit aftermarket alarms and immobilisers as well. But it's still relatively quick for an experienced gang to lift a bike into the back of an anonymous van and make a speedy getaway.

Fortunately, there are things you can do to make life more difficult for them. A hefty chain and padlock is low tech compared to the latest generation of electronic alarms, but it means you can chain your bike to an immovable object. It's also a highly visible deterrent, and picking the lock or breaking the chain will take time and attract attention. But heavy-duty chains are – there's no getting away from the fact – heavy. They'll take up valuable luggage room too, but as a security feature they're highly effective.

Where you park the bike will have a great effect on how vulnerable it is, especially overnight. When looking for accommodation, ask if the hotel has a private car park, out of sight of the road. In the Third World, some hotel owners are happy for you to wheel your bike into reception overnight, while others have gated courtyards that keep it out of sight. A lone bike, parked by the kerb overnight, is in the most vulnerable spot of all. If you have to leave the bike out, park it next to other bikes or cars, or next to a wall, so that it's less conspicuous.

During the day, the busiest areas are the most secure places to park. Avoid deserted car parks or odd corners in the more industrial districts. Amid the crowds of a shopping area, parked up with a row of other bikes, your machine stands a better chance of blending in. Of course, even that's no guarantee of safety. I once parked an electric scooter in a busy shopping street, and turned round after walking 100 metres to see three young boys calmly wheeling it away! They didn't keep it for long.

The same applies to the security of your luggage. Keep valuables either in your jacket or the tankbag, and when you leave the bike, unzip the tankbag and take it with you – some bags have a smaller section that can be unzipped separately and is more convenient to carry. If you've stopped for lunch, try and find a café from which you can keep an eye on the bike.

All this talk of security can make one paranoid, and applying commonsense security measures shouldn't blind us to the fact that the vast majority of people would not dream of stealing anything at all.

Keep money secure

If you need to carry cash, hide it in smaller wads, so that if the worst happens you aren't likely to lose the lot. Carry two wallets, one for regular use (with a closed credit card and a small amount of ready cash) the other well hidden for bigger bills. A wallet-to-belt chain is a good idea, and if you use a money belt, wrap the money in plastic so that it's not damaged by sweat, a rainstorm or falling off in a river.

113

Lockable topbox, good news, unlockable soft panniers, not so good. Helmets can be locked to the bike though

If you want to find a good mechanic, ask a local motorcyclist

Breakdowns

Assuming you have breakdown cover (see page 80), the most important thing to think about if the bike does splutter to a halt is keeping safe. Wheel the bike off the road if at all possible, or at least away from any bends. On motorways, wait for help up on the verge, not down by the bike. You may be there for some time, so take a bottle of water and a good book with you. As in Britain, there are emergency phones in most countries, though in Europe you may have mobile coverage anyway. When you do get going again, don't forget the golden rule about leaving the hard shoulder – let your speed build up to match that of the traffic before rejoining the carriageway.

Modern bikes are very reliable, so the most common causes of 'breakdowns' are running out of fuel, or a puncture. In the latter case, if you have the tools, a centre stand and the inclination, it will save time to remove the wheel before the breakdown help arrives. Often another motorcyclist will stop in the meantime, to offer help. Local knowledge is a great help, and they should know exactly where the nearest bike shop is.

Road accidents

If you're involved in a crash (even indirectly, as a witness) your first priority is to prevent another accident. Motorists abroad have to carry warning triangles, so ensure these are placed at least 100 metres back from the scene, to warn oncoming vehicles. Everyone should keep off the road (unless attending to casualties who can't be moved) and stay visible.

If anyone is injured (and in some countries if significant damage has been caused) you must by law call the police. For the emergency dialling code see the country by country section of this book, though 112 is widely used in Europe and 911 in North America. Even if no one is hurt and damage appears to be minor, it's a good idea to call the police anyway.

Do not move the vehicles unless they're seriously holding up traffic – moving vehicles in the aftermath of a crash is actually illegal in Turkey. If you have to move anything, take pictures to confirm its post-crash position, and don't leave before the police arrive, even if you're convinced everyone is OK. The same goes for any witnesses. Make a note of the other party's name, address, registration number and insurance company.

As soon as you can, notify your insurance company (they may have an office in the country), and if you have a European Accident Statement, the more details you include with this, including photographs, the better. If you're injured, visit a local doctor to get written confirmation of your injuries and any treatment given – the insurance company will need to know this.

Helping casualties
If you've never been on a first aid course, do so before you go. One ambulance service in the UK is now offering a course specifically aimed at motorcyclists, but any first aid course taught by a professional will do.

Casualties should not be moved unless there is an urgent need to do so, and people with minor injuries may still be suffering from shock, so they need to be kept warm – if no one has a blanket, your bike jacket over their shoulders will do – and should not be left alone.

If a motorcyclist is injured, do not attempt to remove their helmet unless they're choking or not breathing. Trying to take the helmet off can aggravate a neck injury, but if you have to do so in order to resuscitate, get someone to support the head and neck while you gently remove the lid.

Medical basics
Don't forget to take a basic first aid kit – even if you aren't confident in using it, someone else probably will be – along with aspirin and diarrhoea blockers.

115

First Aid training can prove invaluable in a post-crash situation, as even quite simple techniques can save lives

RIDING IN
WESTERN
EUROPE

When we first venture abroad by bike, mainland Western Europe is usually our destination. It's easier to get to by bike from the UK than anywhere else (a quick ferry trip or 35 minutes on Le Shuttle), and there's the comforting thought that if anything does go wrong, home isn't far away.

117

The English Channel is a psychological barrier, but once we make that leap there's a whole world of touring opportunity on the mainland: the Alps, the Mediterranean coast, the forests and lakes of Germany, the Spanish Picos de Europa and Italy's beautiful Adriatic coast.

These varied attractions underline the fact that Western Europe is not one country, but a whole series, which brings challenges of its own. Speed limits vary from place to place, as do road signs and priority rules. Border controls might be a thing of the past, but language and culture still changes when you enter a new country. And while this vista begins just 35 minutes from Dover, it's still 'abroad', so you need to check that all your paperwork is in order, that you have proper insurance cover and a valid, stamped European Health Insurance Card. Finally, it's worth remembering that Britain and Ireland remain the odd men out in Europe: everyone else drives on the right.

As Britain's closest 'abroad,' mainland Europe is a good venue for a first-time tour

A Russian bike in the former East Germany; heading for Berlin, but outside the city, there were still signs of the old Iron Curtain regime

Biker's Tale – Germany
Peter Henshaw

It seemed like a good idea at the time. Ride a Russian-built Ural to Berlin and what was left of the Wall. Not only was the Ural built in the former Soviet Union, but it was based on a pre-war BMW design that the Russians bought from the Germans back in 1938, when those two ideologically opposed nations were temporarily friends.

I'd never been east of what used to be the Iron Curtain, but this was 2003, 13 years after Berliners put an end to that whole geo-political nonsense by dancing on top of the famous Wall. Surely after 13 years the old East Germany would have caught up with the affluent West? I stopped at the old border post just east of Lauenburg – no guards, no gate, just an old concrete office block that was clearly someone's house now, washing billowing in the wind. A man watched me out of a window – I waved, and he nodded back.

We kept to Route 5, the old main road between Hamburg and Berlin. This used to be one of the few permitted road routes between the West and Berlin, but now it's very quiet, bypassed by a new motorway. The road runs through a bleak, flat agricultural landscape, and here there was a sense of difference from the West. There were signs of change: a brand new John Deere tractor trundling between the fields; a modern wind farm on the horizon; and workmen erecting new crash barriers at the roadside.

But the villages along Route 5 had a shabby, abandoned air about them, as if the population had left in search of greener pastures – a lot of them probably had. Passing one farmhouse at the Ural's steady 50mph, I noticed a shiny VW Golf sitting outside, but in the barn next door was a cobwebbed Trabant, quietly decaying. The first thing most Ossies did after reunification, a German friend told me, was to buy a new car.

The closer we got to Berlin, the more obvious the changes were. Out-of-town shopping centres, a new motorway, and Western levels of traffic. Route 5 is an atmospheric route into the old German capital – it runs in a straight line right up to the foot of the Brandenberg Gate, rather like the old A4 takes you from Bristol all the way to Hyde Park Corner. Over the next couple of days, I was moved by the Checkpoint Charlie Museum, and by the new Jewish Museum on Linden Strasse. Behind the crowded cafés and upmarket hotels, new office blocks were springing up next to a crumbling concrete watchtower – the contrast between the old Berlin and the new couldn't have been more stark.

On my last night in Germany, I rode 20 miles west of Berlin, past the pavement cafés, the shopping centres and motorways, to the town of Nauen. Suddenly, I was back in the real East Germany, which had yet to be touched by the new affluence. Next morning, I woke up to see nearly every chimney smoking, as the population stoked up their coal fires. I climbed back onto the Ural, and headed west.

Outdated? Of course, but the Ural proved well up to a 600-mile round trip through Germany and Denmark

FRANCE

Not all roads lead to Paris, and France offers a hugely varied choice of tarmac, people and topography

If you're looking to take your bike abroad for the first time, France is undoubtedly a good choice of destination. For a start, it's our closest neighbour, and for most British riders the easiest European country to get to. Easiest of all for those living in London and the south-east, where the Channel Tunnel offers a quick and efficient alternative to the short Dover-Calais ferry ride. For access to western France, take a longer crossing from Plymouth, Poole or Portsmouth.

France is a big country, but whichever entry port you use there's good access to a huge variety of attractions – Bordeaux, Brittany and the French Alps are all within a day's ride of the Channel, if you don't mind sticking to the autoroutes, though you'll have to be pretty determined to reach the Mediterranean coast in a day.

On the road

One of the best ways to appreciate France is not to be too ambitious about distance, but stick to the quiet D and N roads (the equivalent of our Bs and As), pass through the towns and villages, and stop where you like. You can actually make quite good time on the straight, tree-lined Routes Nationales. Use your time on the ferry to trace a suitable route, or use the Bison Futé (crafty bison) or Bis routes, which keep to the more picturesque main roads – a free map of these can be picked up at tourist offices and some filling stations.

Of course, if you do want to just get somewhere

fast, the French autoroutes are smooth, well maintained, and have a 130kph (80mph) limit. A péage (toll) is payable, but it's a very simple system – you just take a ticket from a machine as you enter and hand it to a cashier when you leave. You can pay by cash or credit card. Bikes pay about half the rate of cars, and riding from Calais to Paris costs around €10. The autoroutes are also well supplied with rest areas (glorified lay-bys with grass and picnic benches) every 10km or so and service areas every 30-40km.

Small hotels are easy to find in most French towns and villages, reasonably priced and with personal service. If you're sticking to the autoroutes, one of the chains of cheap, basic hotels, such as Formule 1, should deliver an efficient night's rest.

Rules of the road

Perhaps the most important difference between French and British motoring law – apart from driving on the right – is *priorité au droite* (give way to the right). Unless there are signs to the contrary, vehicles entering from the right always have right of way, even if they're joining a main road. So watch out when riding through town. The same rule applies to many roundabouts (including the monstrous race track around the Arc de Triomphe in Paris), though these are increasingly changing to the British system. If so, the *Vous n'avez pas la priorité* sign is the one to look for, or *Cedéz le passage*. If the main road you're on displays a yellow diamond sign, then it has priority over side roads.

If you're 17, then prepare for disappointment. Most European countries insist that you cannot ride a motorcycle until you are 18, and France is no exception. It doesn't matter that your full bike licence is legal in Britain – it won't be legal in France until you're 18. Even then, a lower speed limit applies until you've held your licence for two years – 100kph (62mph) on dual carriageways, 110kph (68mph) on motorways. These lower limits also apply to everyone in wet weather.

Priority road

Priority road ends

Give way

Restriction continues

Traffic already on roundabout has right of way

Stop at toll booth

FRANCE

Speed limits

Speaking of speed limits, in Britain we're used to large, clear '30' or '40' signs at the start of every town or village, but in France there's often just the place name sign: the urban speed limit starts there, and ends when you see the name sign crossed out. The French police are hot on speeding, and anyone caught exceeding the limit by 40kph (25mph) can have their photocard driving licence confiscated on the spot. You then face the problem of getting your bike home again. Radar detectors are also illegal, even if they're not being used – once again, the penalties can be heavy. The detector will be confiscated, you'll have to pay a deposit on a large fine, and a court summons will follow. Your bike may be confiscated as well.

The drink-drive limit in France is the Euro-average of 50mg/100ml, and the penalties for exceeding it include fines, imprisonment and confiscation of your driving licence. It's always tempting in this wine-drinking culture to have a glass of red with lunch – it's safer to stick to mineral water, though. In addition saliva tests were introduced in 2005 to check drivers and riders thought to be under the influence of drugs. On-the-spot fines, for a number of offences, are severe. You should be given an official receipt.

Paris

Finally, if you're used to riding in city traffic then Paris shouldn't be too daunting. The Peripherique can be scary – junctions are frequent and (unlike the M25) traffic is often moving at a pace – but the French capital is full of bikes and scooters. There's plenty of two-wheel parking, and it's a great part of a touring holiday to park up, sit outside a pavement café and be part of Parisian motorcycle culture.

Parisian traffic is a stimulating experience on two wheels

RIDING IN **WESTERN** EUROPE

FACT FILE FRANCE

Speed limits	Urban	Open road	Motorway
Motorcycle	50kph	90kph	110-130kph
Wet weather	50kph	80kph	100-110kph
Traffic regulations			
Minimum driving age	18yrs		
Drink-drive limit	50mg alcohol per 100ml blood		
Helmets	Compulsory		
Daytime lights	Compulsory		
Emergency telephone numbers			
Police	17		
Fire	18		
Ambulance	15		
Useful phrases			
Allumez vos lanternes	Switch on headlights		
Attention travaux	Roadworks ahead		
Chaussée déformée	Poor road surface		
Déviation	Diversion		
Gravillons	Loose chippings		
Parking payant	Charge for parking		
Péage	Road toll		
Ralentissez	Slow down		
Rappel	Restriction (such as speed limit) continues		
Route barrée	Road closed		
Stationnement interdit	No parking		

LUXEMBOURG

It can take barely 25 minutes to cross Luxembourg on the motorway (it's 32 miles across at its widest point) and consequently most riders give a barely a second thought to it as they race eastwards into Germany, or back west for the Channel ports. Even for French and German drivers, the little country's main attraction seems to be that fuel is slightly cheaper there, so that many nip over the border to fill up.

But the Duchy of Luxembourg deserves more than that. The north and west of the country include part of the Ardennes, and Luxembourg city is named the 'Gibraltar of the north' because of its heavy fortifications dating back hundreds of years. These include a 23km labyrinth of tunnels, in which battalions of troops could eat, sleep and live while defending the city. Luxembourg is also proud of its culinary tradition, said to combine French finesse with German heartiness – if you fancy pike in Riesling sauce, or Ardennes ham, come to the Duchy.

Bilingual
Pillion passengers must be aged at least 12 in Luxembourg and bikes must use dipped headlights in daytime. The motorway speed limit is cut from 120kph (74mph) to 110kph (69mph) in wet weather, and if you've held your licence for less than a year you're restricted to 75kph (46mph) whatever road you're on. The drink-drive limit is the same as in Britain (80mg/100ml) and fines or imprisonment will follow a transgression. The police can impose on-the-spot fines for other offences.

Traffic signs are posted in both French and German, and one extra regulation is that you have to flash your lights before overtaking at night outside built-up areas.

FACT FILE LUXEMBOURG

Speed limits	Urban	Open road	Motorway
Motorcycle	50kph	90kph	120kph
(riders who have held a driving licence for less than one year must not exceed 75kph)			
Traffic regulations			
Essential equipment	Warning triangle		
Minimum driving age	17yrs		
Drink-drive limit	80mg alcohol per 100ml blood		
Helmets	Compulsory		
Daytime lights	Compulsory		
Emergency telephone numbers			
Police	113		
Fire	112		
Ambulance	112		
Useful phrases			
See France and Germany			

Good things come in small packages, or so the Luxembourg tourist board would have us believe

NETHERLANDS

Home zone

Cycle path

Parking blue zone

Park and ride

Compulsory route for hazardous goods

Maximum speed limit

No entry for motorcycles

At first sight the Netherlands doesn't look like a great place for motorcycling – it's a small, flat country, far from the mountainous open spaces of some parts of Europe. But it does have the unique experience of dyke-top roads, which run along the top of the country's sea defences. About ten metres above the ground, these offer open bends and superb views, and it's possible to ride for many miles, rarely dropping below roof level.

Given the popularity of cycling in the Netherlands (there are 12 million bicycles in the country, nearly as many as there are people) you might think that congestion wouldn't be a problem, but the country also has the highest traffic density in Europe.

Changed priorities

In Britain, cyclists still suffer a little from car-drivers' 'might is right' syndrome on the road, but Dutch road users are expected to treat them with courtesy. Home zones, where cyclists and pedestrians have priority over vehicles, are also more common in Holland than here. Buses and trams too have greater priority over cars than in Britain. You must always give way to buses as they pull away in a built-up area, and trams always have priority, even when crossing a major road. They can be overtaken, but usually on the right only – they can be passed on the other side if there is insufficient room on the right, but with caution. In either case, passengers getting on or off the tram have priority over your desire to overtake.

The limits

You have to be aged at least 18 to ride a motorcycle here (even if you're just on holiday from the UK) and the drink-driving limit is 50mg/100ml, with severe penalties – up to imprisonment – if you exceed it. Speed limits are similar to those in Britain, and the police can levy on-the-spot fines.

FACT FILE NETHERLANDS

Speed limits	Urban	Open road	Motorway
Motorcycle	50kph	80-100kph	120kph
Traffic regulations			
Minimum driving age	18yrs		
Drink-drive limit	50mg alcohol per 100ml blood		
Helmets	Compulsory		
Daytime lights	Optional		
Emergency telephone numbers			
Police	112		
Fire	112		
Ambulance	112		
Useful phrases			
Doorgaand verkeer gestremd	No throughway		
Langzaam rijden	Slow down		
Opspattend grind	Loose chippings		
Pas op!	Attention		
Rechtsaf toegestaan	Right turn allowed		
Stop-verbod	No parking		
Tegenliggers	Traffic from opposite direction		
Wegomlegging	Detour		
Werk in uitvoering	Work in progress		

The Dutch are good at pastries, cheese and windmills, and the dyke-top roads are pretty good too

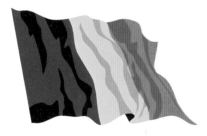

BELGIUM

 Overtake on left or right

 Give way to cyclists crossing side road

 No parking from 1st to 15th of each month

 End of home zone

In France, one of the worst insults a driver can make is Il conduit comme un Belge (he drives like a Belgian). It seems odd that the motorists of this inoffensive little country in northern Europe should have such a bad reputation, but it's based on fact – Belgium has a very high road casualty rate by Western European standards.

Maybe this stems from some deep-seated psychosis (Belgium has a long history of being invaded by powerful neighbours), but the country was also one of the last in Europe to introduce a compulsory driving test, which is no doubt more relevant. There are also many foreign drivers living in Brussels, which probably doesn't help. But keep an eye on the drivers, and Belgium offers the rolling, wooded hills of the Ardennes, some nice twisty roads, and superb restaurants.

Priority on right
Like France, Belgium has a give way to the right rule, and this is what often catches out visiting riders. Even if you're on what appears to be the main road, you have to be ready for cars joining from the right without giving way. If joining a main road from the right, take care you're not rear-ended by the car behind, who may expect you to just sweep into the traffic. As in the Netherlands, trams always have priority.

Two languages
French is spoken in the south of Belgium, and Flemish in the north, and this extends to the road signs. Which can be confusing, because even some of the towns have different names in each language, so your destination can change its name when you cross the linguistic divide.

Road signs
Examples (French name / Flemish name) include:

Liege – Luik
Ypres – Ieper
Lille – Rijsel
Mons – Bergen
Tournai – Doornik
De Han – Le Coq
Kortrijk – Courtrai
Veurne – Furnes
Zouteeuw – Léau.

Brussels, given its status within the EU, has bi-lingual road signs.

FACT FILE BELGIUM

Speed limits	Urban	Open road	Motorway
Motorcycle	50kph	90kph	120kph
Traffic regulations			
Minimum driving age	18yrs		
Drink-drive limit	50mg alcohol per 100ml blood		
Helmets	Compulsory		
Daytime lights	Compulsory		
Emergency telephone numbers			
Police	101		
Fire	100		
Ambulance	100		
Useful phrases			
See France and Netherlands			

Belgian drivers have a bad reputation, but there are quiet corners and superb roads that repay a visit by bike

GERMANY

Lower speed limit applies in the wet

Expressway

One way street

Keep distance shown

Bus or tram stop

If bikers know one thing about Germany, it's that the dense network of *Autobahnen* (motorways) have no speed limits. Unfortunately for those desperate to find out whether their Hayabusa really will touch 200mph, this is not quite the speedfest it might seem.

There is a recommended overall limit of 130kph (80mph), plus other limits at motorway junctions and service areas. German motorways are often two-lane and heavily used, so in practice (especially at holiday times) the opportunity for high speed is quite limited. If you're not interested in riding fast, bear in mind that if you pull into the overtaking lane at 60-70mph, a 150mph Mercedes can be upon you in less time than you could possibly imagine.

On the road

In keeping with the stereotypes of an orderly, disciplined nation, German roads are very well surfaced and maintained, in the East as well. The same goes for German drivers, who show great respect for urban speed limits.

In towns, one traffic rule inherited from the East is that you're permitted to turn right at red traffic lights, where a green arrow is displayed on the traffic lights and you've stopped to check that the way is clear first. Traffic lights are often turned off at night, in which case you go by the stop or give way signs also displayed. Congestion is often serious, but flow is aided by the zipper rule (*Reissverschluss*), meaning cars give way one at a time at junctions or where two lanes merge into one.

What to see

Germany has, to use that hackneyed tour-guide phrase, something for everyone. Vineyards and deep valleys in the Moselle; the mountainous south merging into Austria; the eastern plains stretching to Berlin and beyond; and the lakes and schlosses of the Baltic coast. If you want to avoid the long motorway haul from the French ferry ports, take the Harwich-Hamburg boat instead.

FACT FILE GERMANY

Speed limits	Urban	Open road	Motorway
Motorcycle	50kph	100kph	130kph *(recommended)*
Traffic regulations			
Minimum driving age	18yrs		
Drink-drive limit	50mg alcohol per 100ml blood		
Helmets	Compulsory		
Daytime lights	Compulsory		
Emergency telephone numbers			
Police	112		
Fire	112		
Ambulance	112		
Useful phrases			
Achtung	Attention		
Ausfahrt	Exit		
Bei Nässe	In wet weather		
Gefahr	Danger		
Licht einschalten	Turn on headlamps		
Ölspur	Oil on road		
Parkplatz	Parking lot		
Rasthof	Service area		
Rollsplitt	Loose chippings		
Schlechte wegstrecke	Uneven road		
Stau	Traffic congestion		
Tankstelle	Filling station		
Vorfahrt	Right of way		

AUSTRIA

 Umleitung *Diversion*

 Buses only

Street lights not lit all night long

 Tram may turn on red or amber

Austria, with its Alpine landscape and terrific, twisty roads, is a bit of a motorcyclists' mecca. Bikers from Germany and Italy will nip over the border at weekends for a quick blast, and it makes a great touring destination from Britain. Best experience: sipping a cappuccino at the top of a mountain pass, watching the bikes wind their way up hairpin after hairpin towards you. Don't forget Vienna, for its culture, architecture and serious cream cakes.

Austria is a long ride away from Britain (it's around 800 miles from London to Salzburg), so unless you're prepared to put in some serious miles on the way down, the country is best taken as part of a longer two-week tour.

On the road

Austrian roads are well surfaced and nicely maintained, though the Alpine hotspots will get congested in summer. On the narrower mountain roads, be prepared to give way to buses, and the rule with other traffic is that the vehicle that can stop most easily (whether going up or down) must do so.

To use Austrian motorways you have to purchase and display a vignette, and this applies to bikes as well as cars. Available at border crossings and filling stations, they are valid for ten days, two months or a year, and the motorcycle rate is around half that for cars. Even with a vignette, you'll still have to pay a toll on some tunnels, but you will get a 15 per cent discount. Try riding on a motorway without a vignette and you could be in for a heavy fine.

The police can impose on-the-spot fines, and exceeding the 50mg/100ml drink-drive limit can involve both a fine and a riding ban. You have to be aged at least 18 to ride a motorcycle in Austria.

FACT FILE AUSTRIA

Speed limits	Urban	Open road	Motorway
Motorcycle	50kph	100kph	130kph*
	110kph limit applies on some motorways at night		
Traffic regulations			
Minimum driving age	18yrs		
Drink-drive limit	50mg alcohol per 100ml blood		
Helmets	Compulsory		
Daytime lights	Compulsory		
Emergency telephone numbers			
Police	112		
Fire	112		
Ambulance	112		
Useful phrases			
Hupverbot	No horn use allowed		
Glatteisgefahr	Icy road		
Lawinen Gefahr	Danger of avalanche		
Steinschlag	Falling rocks		
Verengte Fahrbahn	Road narrows		

Austria is a favourite destination for thousands of riders, and it's not difficult to see why

SWITZERLAND

Tunnel (lights compulsory)

Level crossing

Single-carriageway motorway

Blue zone parking

Slow lane

Forget the cuckoo clocks and chocolate: the best thing about Switzerland has to be its spectacular scenery and the roads that run through it. The country has an excellent public transport system as well, but you didn't ride all this way to catch a bus, did you? Having said that, it's good to know it's there, and a Swiss mountain railway is a good stress-free means of peak bagging, if you fancy a day off the bike.

On the road

On those narrow mountain roads, the rule is to give way to vehicles coming up, and you must always give way to mail vans. Some small roads are one-way, but the direction of flow changes according to time of day. Swiss roads can get congested, especially in summer, and if you find yourself sitting in a jam at a tunnel or border crossing you must switch your engine off.

It's illegal to carry a radar detector (even if it's not switched on), and exceeding the drink-drive limit (50mg/100ml) brings severe penalties including a fine or prison sentence. Foreign riders may also be forbidden from riding in Switzerland for at least two months. You need to be at least 18 to ride a bike over 125cc here, and the police can impose on-the-spot fines, though not for everything.

Give way

Like France, Switzerland has a give way to the right rule, except on main roads signed with a yellow diamond. Buses pulling out have priority and road signs come in French, German or Italian. You will need a vignette to use Swiss motorways, but it's only available for a full 14 months and motorcycles pay the same rate as cars – so it's better to stay off the motorways altogether.

FACT FILE SWITZERLAND

Speed limits	Urban	Open road	Motorway
Motorcycle	50kph	80-100kph	120kph
Traffic regulations			
Minimum driving age	18yrs		
Drink-drive limit	80mg alcohol per 100ml blood		
Helmets	Compulsory		
Daytime lights	Compulsory		
Emergency telephone numbers			
Police	117		
Fire	118		
Ambulance	144		
Useful phrases			
See France, Germany and Italy			

Craggy mountains and spectacular passes are what Switzerland has to offer. And did we mention the chocolate?

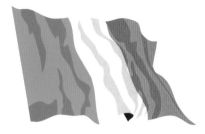

IRELAND

Straight ahead only

Parking permitted

Roundabout

Give way

Dip in road ahead

Unguarded level crossing

Road narrows

Everything you've heard about Ireland is true, and even more so the further west you go. With its beautiful countryside and laid back pace of life, it's perfect for a relaxed tour. For anyone nervous about riding on mainland Europe, here they drive on the left and everyone speaks English. But officially, Ireland is a foreign country, so all your paperwork has to be just as it would be for a trip to France or Italy.

On the road
Ireland has embarked on a big road improvement programme recently, but motorways and dual carriageways are still rare outside Dublin. Traffic is light though, and it doesn't seem to matter too much. So main roads are usually two-lane blacktop, with a broken yellow line separating the hard shoulder from the main carriageway. You're expected to pull over onto the shoulder if someone faster wants to overtake.

Minor roads (Irish R roads are equivalent to our B roads) have more uneven surfaces, and you may find livestock wandering over them in rural areas. Towns and villages tend not to be bypassed, but this is a plus, giving you the opportunity to stop somewhere more interesting for lunch.

Distances are measured in kilometres on road signs, though these intermingle with older signs in miles. Speed limits are now shown in kilometres per hour. As in the UK, there's a 80mg/100ml drink-driving limit. It's compulsory to use the headlight in daytime.

Where to go
Irish scenery is tranquil rather than spectacular, though it does get more exciting as you head west, and the Wicklow Mountains south of Dublin have a couple of nice routes. On the west coast, the Ring of Kerry is a well known scenic circuit, and can get crowded in the summer – also try the circuit around the Beara Peninsula, and the narrow one-way road around the Dingle Peninsula. If you have more time, the north has some superb coast roads as well.

FACT FILE IRELAND

Speed limits	Urban	Open road	Motorway
Motorcycle	50kph	100kph	120kph
Traffic regulations			
Minimum driving age	18yrs		
Drink-drive limit	80mg alcohol per 100ml blood		
Helmets	Compulsory		
Daytime lights	Compulsory		
Emergency telephone numbers			
Police	999 / 112		
Fire	999 / 112		
Ambulance	999 / 112		

Quiet roads and a tranquil landscape are Irish specialities

RIDING IN
SCANDINAVIA

If the great outdoors and spectacular scenery is your bag, then you need to head for Scandinavia. This is river deep, mountain high country, with soaring peaks, deep fjords and dense forests. With little industry or population, the air is clean, fresh and clear. And in summer, the far north has the attraction of virtually 24-hour daylight. All of it is just a ferry ride away from the UK.

Iceland and the Scandinavian countries aren't the place for speeding. There's a strong road safety culture, so speed limits are low and strictly policed, as is drink-driving. Scandinavian drivers tend to be careful, conscientious and law abiding. The same isn't true of the wildlife, and elk or reindeer are a serious hazard in the more remote areas, especially at dawn and dusk.

Riding at these northern latitudes can also be a chilly affair, even in summer, and habitation is sparsely spread, but the views will make it all worthwhile.

139

Spectacular scenery and clean air are the attraction of Scandanavia – if you want to ride fast, go elsewhere

Iceland: where else can you see volcanic mudpools one day, and a glacial lagoon the next? Just watch out for the end of the tarmac

Biker's tale – Iceland
Peter Henshaw

Iceland is a stunning country, and the best way to see it is to ride up to Aberdeen and catch the Shetland ferry. From there, you jump on to the giant MV Norrona – more cruise liner than ferry – which takes you on to Iceland via the Faeroes. You're effectively at sea for three days, but it adds another dimension to the whole trip and certainly beats sitting on a plane for a few hours.

I did have a moment of trepidation as we boarded the Norrona, though. Of the 20-odd bikes boarding with us, most were butch-looking BMW GSs, Honda Africa Twins and KTMs with knobbly tyres. Their riders wore off-road body armour and serious faces. Our Yamaha TDM was one of just two road bikes on board. I'd heard that not all Icelandic roads were tarmacked – perhaps we'd been too ambitious?

But we needn't have worried. Even those sections of Route 1 (Iceland's main road that circles the island) that aren't tarmacked have hard-packed gravel. On just a couple of sections it was loose enough to allow the heavily-laden TDM to start wandering around, but a bit of extra gas got us safely through. Serious off-road bikers head straight across the interior, where the 'roads' are unsurfaced tracks, there are rivers to ford, and no filling stations to speak of.

There's a blanket 90kph (56mph) speed limit in Iceland, but very little traffic, and riding here is quite unlike anything in Europe. Even on this main road, we didn't see a car for ten minutes at a time as we passed through the moon-like landscape in the north-east of the island – early US astronauts actually came here to practice moon walking. Past the volcanic country around Lake Myvatn, with its extraordinary rock formations, and on to the port of Akureyri. That was as far north as we got.

Some people do the entire 1,800-mile round trip of Route 1 in a week (when the ferry comes back to pick you up) but that's quite an intense trip, especially on a bike. We wanted time to stop and look around, so we spent a day whale-watching in Husavik before heading back south. Iceland is nothing if not varied, and on its southern edge we gazed at Jokulsarlen (Europe's largest glacier), took an amphibious bus through a glacial lagoon, and sat on a black-sand beach in T-shirts as the sun shone.

Iceland is incredible to see by bike, and a ferry is the best way to get there. I suppose we could have flown out in a fraction of the time, and done a coach trip, but what plane allows you to look up from your breakfast, and see whales 100 metres away?

The Icelandic ferry gives you a compulsory stop-over in the Faeroes on the way home, for more waterfalls and green mountains. Roast puffin is on the menu

ICELAND

This mid-Atlantic island isn't everyone's first choice for a motorcycle holiday, simply because, being halfway to Canada, it's a very long way off. You can fly of course, and hire a car or take a coach trip, but then you'd be missing out on a three-day mini-cruise at each end, plus the joy of riding your own bike around this extraordinary place.

On the road

Riding across Iceland's interior is for experienced off-road riders only. Not only is the terrain tricky – rivers are forded rather than bridged – but the area is remote, with very little traffic, so if you break down you'll have a long wait.

Even on the main Route 1, you need to be reasonably confident about riding on gravel, which you'll encounter between the ferry port of Seyoisfjorour (in the far east of the island) and the capital Reykjavik (in the far west). Note that a lower 80kph (50mph) speed limit applies on the gravel sections. Bike dealers will only be found in the capital.

Iceland is an expensive place to visit. Petrol costs of over £1 per litre might not seem too bad, but hotel accommodation is particularly steep, though you can cut costs by opting for a youth hostel (of which there are several) or camping. For bikers, this is a summer-only destination, when the temperature is comfortable, though you'll probably still see some rain.

Weather

If heading for the more remote parts, always fill up with fuel first, unless your bike has a 200-mile plus range. Most filling stations accept credit cards, and there are ATMs in most towns (though these are far apart).

The police can impose on-the-spot fines, but you'll usually have to pay up at a police station or into an official account. There's a drink-driving limit of 50mg/100ml, with severe penalties for anyone caught exceeding it.

FACT FILE ICELAND

Speed limits	Urban	Gravel	Tarmac
Motorcycle	50kph	80kph	90kph
Traffic regulations			
Minimum driving age	17yrs		
Drink-drive limit	50mg alcohol per 100ml blood		
Helmets	Compulsory		
Daytime lights	Compulsory		
Emergency telephone numbers			
Police	112		
Fire	112		
Ambulance	112		
Useful phrases			
Bannað að stöðava ökutæki	No stopping		
Framúrakstur bannaður	No overtaking		
Hægið á ykkur	Slow down		
Hættuleg beygja	Dangerous bend		
Hjáleið	Diversion		
Innakstur bannað ur	One-way traffic		
Lögregla	Police station		
Steinkast	Loose chippings		
Útskot	Passing place		
Vegavinna	Roadworks		

Summer is the only practical time to visit Iceland or the Faeroes – even then, views like this aren't guaranteed

DENMARK

Traffic merges

Minimum speed limit

Advisory speed limit

Place of interest

1 hour parking zone

Denmark is a great place for relaxed touring. It's a small country, with a good network of well-surfaced roads connecting long stretches of coastline with rolling hills and inland lakes. Drivers are relaxed too, and as a measure of the Danes' consideration for others, when the roads are slushy they are required to slow down to avoid splashing cyclists, pedestrians and mopeds!

On the road

Danish motorways are toll-free, but given the relatively short distances they're not essential routes. The exception is the spectacular ten-mile motorway bridge between Zealand (location of the capital Copenhagen) and all routes to Jutland (Denmark's mainland). Otherwise, the Marguerite Routes are highly recommended, around 2,000 miles of quiet minor roads that pass through scenic areas or past tourist attractions. Look for the signs – a white daisy on a brown background.

Getting there

To reach Denmark, you can take the direct DFDS ferry from Harwich, though this needs booking well in advance. Or you could ride overland through France and/or Germany.

Apart from the motorways, speed limits are quite low – 80kph (50mph) on the open road – and on-the-spot fines are levied on tourists. These vary greatly with the offence, from just a few hundred krone for 20kph (12mph) over, to several thousand if you do silly speeds on a motorway. Drink-drive violations are dealt with similarly, up to a possible prison sentence.

Cycling is very popular in Denmark, and you may have to give way to cyclists in town. In fact, it makes a nice change to leave the motorcycle for a while and hire a bicycle for a day. Finally, one hint for route finding – roads out of towns and cities are handily named after the town they're heading for, so the road leaving Odense for Faaborg is called Faaborgvej.

FACT FILE DENMARK

Speed limits	Urban	Open road	Motorway
Motorcycle	50kph	80kph	110kph
Traffic regulations			
Essential equipment	Warning triangle		
Minimum driving age	17yrs		
Drink-drive limit	50mg alcohol per 100ml blood		
Helmets	Compulsory		
Daytime lights	Compulsory		
Emergency telephone numbers			
Police	112		
Fire	112		
Ambulance	112		
Useful phrases			
Fare	Danger		
Fodgængerovergang	Pedestrian crossing		
Gennemkørsel forbudt	No through road		
Indkørsel forbudt	No entry		
Korsvej	Crossroads		
Omkørsel	Diversion		
Parkering forbudt	No parking		
Vejen er spærret	Road closed		

Denmark is a typically Scandanavian destination, quite laidback, with quiet roads and low speed limits

SWEDEN

Beware elk

Stop

Tunnel

Slow lane

Sweden is not a top motorcycle destination between December and March, when all the roads are covered with snow and ice (unless you own a sidecar outfit equipped with chains, and are particularly hardy). It's said that this is why many Swedish bikers build such intricate custom bikes – it's to fill the long non-riding winter.

Summer riding

In summer, though, the country can be a rewarding place to tour. Distances are long (Sweden measures 1,500 miles top to bottom as the crow flies, and a lot more by road) and the main roads are straight, passing unvarying countryside. But stick to the twistier minor roads, perhaps concentrating on just one region or nipping over the border into Norway, and you'll find great biking roads plus a wonderful combination of forests, lakes and coastline.

Strict limits

The Swedes are keen drinkers, which could be why the drink driving limit is a low 20mg/100ml. Speed limits are also strictly enforced, and you could have your licence confiscated for breaking the limit by more than 30kph (18mph). The police can impose on-the-spot fines, but you pay them at a post office.

Country roads have little traffic, but you're expected to pull over onto the hard shoulder to let faster traffic past, and on multi-lane roads with a limit of 70kph (44mph) or less overtaking is permitted on both left and right. (Sweden swapped from driving on the left to the right many years ago, literally overnight – it went without a hitch).

Wildlife

The biggest danger for bikers in Sweden isn't any of the above, but the habit of elk, reindeer and other substantial wild animals to wander across the road. Half of the country is forested, so you may not get much warning. Slow down and take care – hitting one of these huge beasts will ruin your holiday.

FACT FILE SWEDEN

Speed limits	Urban	Open road	Motorway
Motorcycle	50kph	70-90kph	110kph
Traffic regulations			
Minimum driving age	18yrs		
Drink-drive limit	20mg alcohol per 100ml blood		
Helmets	Compulsory		
Daytime lights	Compulsory		
Emergency telephone numbers			
Police	112		
Fire	112		
Ambulance	112		
Useful phrases			
Enkelriktat	One way		
Farlig kurva	Dangerous bend		
Grusad väg	Loose chippings		
Höger	Right		
Ingen infart	No entrance		
Parkering förbjuden	No parking		
Polisstation	Police station		
Vänster	Left		
Varning för tåg	Level crossing		

Wandering reindeer are
the main road hazard
in Sweden

NORWAY

Passing place

Bus lane

Lane ends

Traffic joining has priority

Ski runs

Tunnel

Like Sweden, Norway is not worth biking to in the winter – special tyres are mandatory and many roads are closed due to snow. But again like its near neighbour, the reward in summer is good riding along quiet roads through even more spectacular scenery. Deep fjords and high mountains, especially on the west coast, make for a dramatic journey – Norway is unlike anything you'll see in southern Europe.

Ferries run directly from Newcastle to Kristiansand, or indirectly from Aberdeen to Bergen via the Faeroes.

Slow going

Riding anywhere in Norway will take longer than you think. There are frequent tolls on the main roads (often thanks to bridges and tunnels, which are a fact of life in this craggy country), with ferry crossings along the coast. Tolls are also payable on entering cities. Speed limits are low as well – 80kph (50mph) on main roads and 90kph (56mph) on motorways (of which there are few). Limits (both on speed and on drink-driving) are strictly enforced. The police can impose on-the-spot fines, and jail is a possibility for serious transgressions.

Mountain roads

Once off the main roads, Norway's mountain routes can be challenging – they're narrow, and twist and turn over the difficult terrain. Look out for *Møteplass* (meeting points), which are passing places – if there's space on your side, you're obliged to pull in. The reward is a ride through wild, remote country, well away from tourist honeypots.

Filling up

That very remoteness needs thinking about. Filling stations can be miles apart, and not all of them accept credit cards. In fact, heading for the wilder parts of Norway is inadvisable if your bike has a range of 100 miles or less.

FACT FILE NORWAY

Speed limits	Urban	Open road	Motorway
Motorcycle	50kph	80kph	90kph
Traffic regulations			
Minimum driving age	17yrs		
Drink-drive limit	20mg alcohol per 100ml blood		
Helmets	Compulsory		
Daytime lights	Compulsory		
Emergency telephone numbers			
Police	112		
Fire	110		
Ambulance	113		
Useful phrases			
All stans førbudt	No stopping		
Enveiskjøring	One-way traffic		
Ikke møte	No overtaking		
Kjør sakte	Slow down		
Løs grus	Loose chippings		
Møteplass	Passing place		
Omkjøring	Diversion		
Veiarbeide	Roadworks		

East Anglia it's not. In Norway, the roads have to fight their way through mountains and over fjords

FINLAND

Beware reindeer

Detour

No parking: 8am-5pm (Mon-Fri)

No parking: 8am-1pm (Sat)

No parking: 8am-2pm (Sun)

Riding to Finland looks like being beyond the scope of a standard two-week holiday, but it's possible to catch the Newcastle ferry to Gothenburg, then ride across Sweden for the Stockholm-Helsinki boat. The more adventurous (and they'll need more than two weeks) could ride overland through northern Europe and the Baltic states, then cross the border via St Petersburg. Alternatively, riding to Stockholm via Denmark and the Oresund bridge avoids the worry of entering Russia.

Good roads
Despite its place on the very edge of Europe, Finland has a good network of well-maintained roads, none of which carry tolls. There are lots of ferries to help take you across this lake-filled land, but these are free of charge as well. Of course, the frequent ferry crossings dramatically increase journey times, while the usual open road speed limit is just 80kph (50mph).

Give way
It's compulsory to give way to the right at intersections, and to trams and buses pulling out anywhere. Outside built-up areas, elk and reindeer should always be given way to. Joking apart, these are a serious hazard, and if you hit one you'll come off worst. All such collisions must be reported to the police, while accidents involving another road user have to be reported to the Finnish Motor Insurers' Centre (tel: 9-680-401).

Filling up
Filling up with fuel needs thinking about in Finland, especially if you have a small tank. Filling stations can be miles apart in the remote north, and most of them (all over the country) will close at night. Fuel can also be significantly more expensive in the north, though most stations will take credit cards. Don't be tempted to drink and ride in Finland – get caught with more than 20mg/100ml and you'll face a confiscation of your licence and a jail sentence.

FACT FILE FINLAND

Speed limits	Urban	Open road	Motorway
Motorcycle	50kph	80-100kph	120kph
Traffic regulations			
Minimum driving age	18yrs		
Drink-drive limit	50mg alcohol per 100ml blood		
Helmets	Compulsory		
Daytime lights	Compulsory		
Emergency telephone numbers			
Police	112		
Fire	112		
Ambulance	112		
Useful phrases			
Aja hitaasti	Slow down		
Aluerajoitus	Local speed limit		
Lossi-farja	Ferry		
Kelirikko	Road damaged by frost		
Kunnossapitotyo	Roadworks		
Moottoritie	Motorway		

Lake-filled Finland offers a remote and watery landscape that could form part of a longer tour

RIDING IN
SOUTHERN
EUROPE

Even keen riders who are on the road all year round in the UK really look forward to those long summer days when the air is warm and it doesn't take ten minutes to tog up before each ride. If only it were possible to enjoy this every summer. But it is – just head south! Take your pick and enjoy some of Europe's finest biking roads combined with amazing scenery and a population that is very biking orientated.

153

Where to go? East to west are Greece, Italy, the south of France, Spain and Portugal. All are part of Europe's 'Sun Belt', all are steeped in history, have good food and wine, great beaches, and wall to wall sunshine. Accommodation is plentiful and not at all expensive, especially in France. Getting to the sun has never been easier: fast ferries take you direct from Portsmouth or Plymouth to northern Spain. From there you can ride on to Portugal. Going through France gives you access to its Mediterranean resorts; from there Italy beckons and onwards to Greece, the cradle of democracy. The languages and cultures of Southern Europe are diverse, but you'll gain much kudos by making an attempt at the language – it's a great way to break the ice and is appreciated by the locals.

Hot summers and a strong two-wheel culture are the attractions of southern Europe

Typical hilltop town in Spain, and the Honda Pan European is a good bike to see it on

Biker's tale – Spain
Phil Butler

I remember my first year living in Asturias, northern Spain. I spent it discovering some great rides and getting accustomed to life Asturian style. It wasn't just the great roads, the dependable good weather and a whole country that seemed to be motorcycle mad. Asturians have a laidback attitude that appeals even if you're only staying a few days. To see what I mean, read on...

It had been a great run over the mountain from Corrao to Riocaliente, the weather sunny and warm. Without thinking I turned on to a road that would take me home, forgetting that it was closed for resurfacing. A crowd of locals had gathered at the junction – it was a little local ceremony to celebrate the reopening of the road, and I didn't mind waiting a few minutes, so I parked the bike and wandered up to where the action was

At the crossroads, the old ladies of the village had commandeered the shady spots under trees, busily wafting their fans and exchanging gossip, not necessarily in that order of importance. Someone had strung bunting from the trees with the flags of Asturias and Spain interspersed here and there. The road construction crew in their Day-Glo overalls mingled with the villagers, smoking and eyeing up the younger ladies.

Local bar owner José Luis moved to the centre of the crossroads and made a short speech, saying how proud the village was of this beautiful new road and thanking the contractors for their hard work, and so on: 'When the first vehicle arrives at the crossroads the road will be officially open.' José checked his watch. It was two o'clock, but this was Asturias, and traffic wasn't exactly thick on the ground.

Fifteen minutes passed. It was getting hotter, and the men were licking their lips and thinking more of an ice-cold beer than some official ceremony. It was plain that no car was coming. Then I noticed the old basset hound that wanders from village to village. He has no owner, but everyone feeds him, so he lives well and doesn't work for a living like the other dogs.

By now the folks were getting a bit restive – something had to be done. So when Fredo the basset sniffed at the newly laid kerbstones and promptly cocked his leg, someone shouted 'Mira el perro!' ('Look at the dog!') We all clapped and cheered, and José Luis declared that the dog had opened the road. The young girl with the bunch of flowers destined for the driver of the first car solemnly walked to the kerb and placed them where Fredo had been. After that it was free beer and cider in the bar.

Later on I rode home down the refurbished road and there was still no traffic. Why? Because the contractors had forgotten to remove the 'Carreterra Cortada' sign, so the road was still – officially – closed.

A long way from Costa del Chips, northern Spain has the choice of rugged coastline and a mountainous interior

ITALY

Parking restrictions

Snow chains required

No fires permitted

Horizontal traffic light

Stop – police

Apart from Spain, Italy is probably the most motorcycle-orientated country in Europe, so it's a great place to ride a bike. Teenagers on mopeds, leathered-up bikers on a Ducati or a big Japanese sports bike, and just about everyone on a Vespa – two-wheeled transport is part of the social fabric here, and all bikers will wave at you. Better still, this means that most Italian drivers, despite their reputation, are highly aware of two-wheelers.

Naturally, the country is full of superb motorcycling roads, especially in the northern region heading into the Alps (though this can get very crowded in the summer), but if you want to get anywhere fast the autostrada network is highly efficient. Most of these motorways are toll roads, and you can pay by credit card at the toll booth or buy a Viacard from filling stations or tourist offices. The speed limit on some motorways is 150kph (93mph), though you should be aware when pulling out that some cars may be travelling faster than this. In any case, 130kph (just over 80mph) is a more typical limit, and a lower 110kph (69mph) applies in poor weather. The police may use toll tickets to monitor your speed, and on-the-spot fines can be heavy for speeders.

Age limits

We all associate Italy with a free and easy biking culture, yet moped riders now have to wear helmets, and you need to be aged 18 to ride a bike over 125cc. Sub-150cc bikes are not allowed on the autostrada, though that's unlikely to affect anyone who's ridden down from Britain.

When two oncoming vehicles want to turn left at a crossroads, they have to turn in front of each other (not behind, as in Britain). It's worth remembering that the drink-drive limit is stricter than Britain's, at 50mg/100ml, and penalties include confiscation of your bike and imprisonment.

Some filling stations in the more remote areas may not accept credit cards, though on all major roads there shouldn't be a problem.

FACT FILE ITALY

Speed limits	Urban	Open road	Motorway
Motorcycle	50kph	90-110kph	130-150kph
Traffic regulations			
Minimum driving age	18yrs		
Drink-drive limit	50mg alcohol per 100ml blood		
Helmets	Compulsory		
Daytime lights	Compulsory		
Emergency telephone numbers			
Police	112		
Fire	115		
Ambulance	118		
Useful phrases			
Destra	Right		
Incrocio	Crossroads		
Lavori in corso	Roadworks		
Nord	North		
Rallentare	Slow down		
Senso unico	One-way street		
Senso vietato	No entry		
Sinistra	Left		
Sosta vietata	No parking		
Sud	South		
Svolta	Bend or turning		
Tornante	Winding road		
Uscita	Exit		

SPAIN

Accident rate

Spain still has a poor accident rate compared to Britain, especially around the cities and along the busy south coast. The roads are well maintained and the autopista (motorways) mostly toll-free. You no longer need a bail bond to take a vehicle into Spain.

You have to be aged at least 18 to ride anything over 75cc, which discounts 17-year-olds on 125s, and the blood/alcohol limit is 50mg/100ml (30mg for those with less than two years experience). Helmets are only compulsory on bikes of 125cc and over, but riding without one is never worth the risk. And finally, radar detectors are illegal in Spain.

Restricted parking zone

No parking on Monday, Wednesday, Friday or Sunday

No parking on Tuesday, Thursday or Saturday

Use dipped headlamps

Spain is a country where some local bike clubs are funded by the local council, where Moto GP is broadcast live on primetime TV and motorcycles are a way of life. So it's a pretty good region to tour on two wheels, especially if you get away from the crowded 'Costa del Chips' of the south coast. The hot, dry central region, with its straight roads, isn't a great destination, but the mountainous north has much to recommend it.

Take the Picos de Europa, a national park crammed full of mountains (some high enough for a snowline in summer), lakes and gorges. Look at the relevant Michelin map – almost every road in this area has a green line beside it, indicating a scenic route. The bends are endless, and if you want some hairpin practice this is the place to come. If you tire of the mountains, there's a very pleasant Atlantic coastline not far away. Best of all, the Picos are just an hour from the Santander ferry (which runs overnight from Plymouth), and only a little further from the Portsmouth-Bilbao boat.

On the road

Spanish drivers have a reputation for speed and recklessness. They're actually not that bad in lightly trafficked rural areas, but watch out for tailgating if you're cruising gently, looking at the scenery. On single-track roads (of which there are plenty) pull over if a local looms in your mirror, and let them past.

As in France, many Spanish junctions off major roads have an offside pull-in for left turns across oncoming traffic. You have to stop and wait here until both carriageways of the main road are clear. It's a good idea that means you don't have to sit in the middle of a busy road, waiting to turn across the traffic. If no priority is indicated at a junction, give way from the right.

FACT FILE SPAIN

Speed limits	Urban	Open road	Motorway
Motorcycle	50kph	90-100kph	120kph
Traffic regulations			
Minimum driving age	18yrs		
Drink-drive limit	50mg alcohol per 100ml blood		
Helmets	Compulsory (see text)		
Daytime lights	Compulsory		
Emergency telephone numbers			
Police	112		
Fire	112		
Ambulance	112		
Useful phrases			
Abierto	(Road) open		
Carretera de peaje	Toll road		
Ceda el paso	Give way		
Cerrado	(Road) closed		
Despacio	Slow		
Desviación	Detour		
Estación de peaje	Toll station		
Gravilla	Loose chippings		
Obras	Roadworks		
Peligro	Danger		
Prioridad	Right of way		
Prohibición	Prohibited		
Salida	Exit		

PORTUGAL

Like Spain, there's a lot more to Portugal than the crowded coastal holiday resorts. In this case, get away from the Algarve, and the country offers mile after mile of well-maintained, twisting roads through wonderful scenery. You won't find real Alpine-scale mountains, but there's some spectacular topography, and some of the Atlantic coast is almost North Cornish in its ruggedness. The country might seem as if it's on the edge of Europe – and it is – but it's less than a day's ride from the ferry ports of Santander and Bilbao in northern Spain.

On the road

Portugal has a reputation for crazy drivers and crazy-paved roads, with the worst accident record in Europe. But most of the danger zones are around Lisbon and the coastal resorts. Further north, the roads are quieter and drivers more considerate, though in rural areas you do need to be aware of sheep, goats and even horse-drawn carts.

Most of the motorways (auto-estradas) are toll roads, though the booths accept credit cards, as do most filling stations and ATMs.

On-the-spot fines are the rule here, and if you refuse to pay up the police can ultimately confiscate your bike.

No radar detectors

Pillion passengers must be aged over seven, and radar detectors may not be carried or used. A priority from the right rule may apply even if you're on what appears to be the major road. Portugal's drink-driving laws were tightened up recently, and though a trial 20mg limit was dropped (after an outcry from the wine producers) a 50mg limit now applies, with heavier penalties over 80mg. As in Spain, the minimum age to ride a motorcycle (as opposed to a moped) is 18, not 17 as in the UK. Everyone has to carry photographic proof of identity at all times, so if you don't have a photocard driving licence keep your passport with you.

FACT FILE PORTUGAL

Speed limits	Urban	Open road	Motorway
Motorcycle	50kph	90kph	120kph
(riders who have held a licence for less than one year must not exceed 90kph)			
Traffic regulations			
Minimum driving age	18yrs		
Drink-drive limit	50mg alcohol per 100ml blood		
Helmets	Compulsory		
Daytime lights	Compulsory		
Emergency telephone numbers			
Police	112		
Fire	112		
Ambulance	112		
Useful phrases			
Fronteira	Border		
Gasóleo	Diesel		
Itinerário principal	Main road		
Limite de velocidade	Speed limit		
Portagem	Toll		
Sem chumbo	Unleaded petrol		

Get away from the crowded coast, and Portugal has many miles of spectacular roads through mountainous terrain

GREECE

You need to be committed, or on a long tour, to ride to Greece, as it takes a good three days to reach from Britain, even if you stick to motorways. If you can afford to take three weeks off work, it can make a fine destination in a big looping tour of mainland Europe. This should also give you time for a spot of island hopping, making use of the myriad ferries. Most visitors fly, of course.

Greece has a reputation for hiring out death-trap scooters to youngsters with zero riding experience, but things have tightened up recently, and you now have to show at least a category A1 licence (up to 125cc) to hire even a moped.

On the road

As ever with popular holiday destinations, Greek traffic is hectic around the cities and resorts, but venture inland and the roads are much quieter, with just sheep, goats and the odd tourist bus to contend with.

The country has few motorways, and off the major highways the roads can be narrow and twisty, with long drops in mountainous country. Either way, you'll need to allow more time than you might expect to cover long distances.

Go slow

Some locals might not be wearing helmets, but don't be fooled – helmets are now compulsory for all riders of mopeds, scooters and motorcycles in Greece. They all (even riders of big bikes) have to obey lower speed limits than cars. The urban limit for bikes is 40kph (25mph – cars can reach 50kph or 31mph) and on motorways the car limit of 120kph (70mph) is cut to 90kph (55mph). So if you're looking for high speed thrills, go elsewhere. But don't let that put you off – Greece is a fine country to ride though, and you'll experience a wealth of riding on the way there.

FACT FILE GREECE

Speed limits	Urban	Open road	Motorway
Motorcycle	40kph	70kph	90kph
Traffic regulations			
Minimum driving age	17yrs		
Drink-drive limit	50mg alcohol per 100ml blood		
Helmets	Compulsory		
Daytime lights	Compulsory		
Emergency telephone numbers			
Police	100		
Fire	199		
Ambulance	166 *(Athens)*		
Useful phrases			
Αδιεξοδος	Dead end		
Δρόμος κλειστός	Road closed		
Κίνδυνος	Danger		
Ολο δεξιά	Keep right		
Οδικά έργα	Road works ahead		
Απότομος λόφος	Steep hill		
Στροφές	Winding road		

In Greece, keep your eyes open for crumbling roads and apparently schizophrenic road signs

MALTA

No horn blowing

No overtaking by heavy vehicles

Tunnel warning

Hazard at edge of road

Tourist destination

Place name

Just 15 miles across, Malta is not the place to go if you want wide open spaces. But it can make an intriguing stop-off as part of an Italian tour, and there are direct ferries from several Italian and Sicilian ports, so you can take your own bike there quite easily. Why intriguing? Because Malta's long association with Britain has given this Mediterranean island some distinctly British touches, such as red telephone and pillar boxes. They even drive on the left, though the local driving style is more Mediterranean than 1950s Britain.

Small island
Being small, Malta can get congested, especially around the coast, but ride inland and there are some wilder, less populated regions to explore. Jeep safaris are a popular means of doing this, but several dealers also hire bikes at reasonable rates. It's advisable to book these in advance in the summer.

Rules
Maltese speed limits are low, with an 80kph (50mph) limit on the open road – lower limits often apply in tunnels. And as with much of mainland Europe, the minimum age for riding a motorcycle is 18, not 17. If you bring your own bike in by ferry, there's no need for a customs bond if you're staying for less than three months, and a Green Card is not required for EU-registered bikes.

Finally, many Maltese filling stations are closed on Sunday, so fill up on Saturday if you're planning a day out.

FACT FILE MALTA

Speed limits	Urban	Open road	Motorway
Car	50kph	80kph	-
Traffic regulations			
Minimum riding age	18yrs		
Drink-drive limit	80mg alcohol per 100ml blood		
Helmets	Compulsory		
Daytime lights	Not compulsory		
Emergency telephone numbers			
Police	191		
Fire	199		
Ambulance	196		

Malta may not be blessed with far horizons, but it has a unique mix of Mediterranean with touches of old-world England

CYPRUS

With limited ferry access (though you can sail from Greece), Cyprus might not seem like an easy place to go motorcycling, but if you don't want to ride there it's always possible to fly, and hire a bike.

Cyprus has been politically divided between Greek and Turkish jurisdictions since 1974. The southern Republic of Cyprus joined the EU in May 2004, while the Turkish Republic of North Cyprus is still not recognised by the British Government. There has been a thaw in relations between north and south recently though, to the point where tourists can now make day trips across the divide. Take care if exploring the minor roads by bike on your own – it's possible to stray across the border into Turkish Cyprus, and parts are still militarised.

On the road

Cyprus has had a long association with Britain, as a result of which its traffic drives on the left. Be aware that minor roads marked on the map may not be tarmacked, and gravel or dirt can take over without warning, though these are often relatively easy riding.

If you want to enjoy your time on two wheels, the best advice is to steer clear of the crowded coastal resorts and head for the hilly country in the centre of the island, which is a great biking region. Road signs are usually displayed in both Greek and English, and there's a 50kph (31mph) limit in all built-up areas.

Hire a bike

It's easy to hire a bike on the island, and there's quite a good choice on offer. Typical bigger hire bikes include the Honda Shadow 750, Africa Twin, or Suzuki's VX800, but for gentle exploring over shorter distances a smaller machine, such as a 250cc cruiser, will be quite adequate and far cheaper.

You can also hire trail bikes to explore the Trodos mountains, and bike hire in general is plentiful and quite competitive. Hire can be arranged before you go, or when you arrive – as ever, if you're travelling at peak season, pre-booking is best.

FACT FILE CYPRUS

Speed limits	Urban	Open road	Motorway
Motorcycle	50kph	80kph	100kph
Traffic regulations			
Minimum driving age	18yrs		
Drink-drive limit	90mg alcohol per 100ml blood		
Helmets	Compulsory		
Daytime lights	Compulsory		
Emergency telephone numbers			
Police/fire/ambulance	112 or 199		

As with other southern European countries, the best riding in Cyprus is away from the busy coastal resorts, up in the mountains

TURKEY

Turkey has ambitions to build up its tourist trade and join the EU, so bike hire is becoming increasingly popular. But it also has the makings of a true long-distance adventure if you want to ride there, allowing you to dip a toe into the western edge of Asia.

The route through the former Yugoslavia is not recommended, but you can still ride overland via Hungary and Romania. It's just close enough to be the objective of a two-week tour, as long as you're prepared to put in some long days in the saddle. Anyone with an interest in ancient history will find the trip worthwhile.

On the road

Riding in Turkey is quite unlike touring in Europe. Although attitudes to road safety are changing (the police are now getting tough on speed limits) drivers tend to be fast and aggressive, willing to overtake with no margin for error. Ride defensively.

There is an expanding network of motorways, with low tolls, though the booths don't often take plastic and bikes are limited to a lowly 80kph (50mph). Other roads are poorly maintained, and you need to watch out for potholes (plus traffic swerving to avoid them), not to mention unmarked speed humps at the entrance/exit of villages.

You may also come across road blocks at the entrance/exit of urban areas, manned by military police. You need to have all your documents – passport, green card insurance, carnet and registration document – ready for inspection. After dark, watch out for unlit cars, trucks and tractors.

Bike hire

You can always fly to Turkey and hire a bike, everything from a small trail bike to a BMW GS. Guided or solo tours are available, on-road or off. The One More Mile Riders Club (www.ommriders.com) exists to help and advise visiting motorcyclists.

There are plenty of filling stations in Turkey, most of which accept credit cards.

RIDING IN **SOUTHERN** EUROPE

FACT FILE TURKEY

Speed limits	Urban	Open road	Motorway
Motorcycle	50kph	70kph	80kph
Traffic regulations			
Minimum driving age	17yrs		
Drink-drive limit	50mg alcohol per 100ml blood		
Helmets	Compulsory		
Daytime lights	Optional		
Emergency telephone numbers			
Police	155		
Fire	110		
Ambulance	112		
Useful phrases			
Bozuk satıh	Rough surface		
Dikkat	Attention		
Dur	Stop		
Park yapılmaz	No parking		
Tamirat	Roadworks		
Giremez	No entry		
Tek yön	One way		
Yavaş	Slow		
Yaya geçidi	Pedestrian crossing		
Yol kapalı	Road closed		

Turkey can be quite an adventure to ride to (and through) and offers a glimpse of Asia plus ancient history

RIDING IN
EASTERN
EUROPE

Riding through the former Eastern Bloc isn't the adventure it once was, before the fall of the Berlin Wall and the collapse of Communism in Europe. The Baltic states (Latvia, Lithuania and Estonia) plus Poland, the Czech and Slovak Republics, Hungary and Slovenia all joined the EU in May 2004, and all are just two or three days' ride from the Channel ports.

In practice, 15 years after the velvet revolution Eastern Europe remains very different to the West. While some regions are developing fast, others are dependent on low-tech agriculture or have pockets of high unemployment. Roads may be poorly maintained and local vehicles older and poorly lit. These new EU member states should recognise the European Health Insurance Card, but don't rely on it – always have your own medical insurance.

At least one motorcycle tour company has begun to offer guided tours into Russia, but you need to be experienced, and prepared to tackle high-mileage days, to do this.

Eastern Europe hasn't been completely westernised yet, and offers a different touring experience

171

"Crossing into Latvia was tricky." Peter Avard's group found that documentation had to be spot on to cross the border

Biker's tale – Baltic states and Russia

Peter Avard

(Peter and Gloria Avard of MSL Tours led the first organised tour through Eastern Europe to St Petersburg in Russia).

The K1200GT's Bridgestones gripped, slipped and gripped again as we slithered over the wet cobblestones of Riga. It was slippery as hell, as we splashed through dirty brown puddles the size of ponds, and raised tramlines just added to the fun. Behind us were 20-odd adventurous bikers from Britain, on a variety of BMWs, Pan Euros and FJR Yamahas. We'd done our research, but hadn't reccied the route, so our 3,800-mile tour of the former Eastern Bloc was a ride into the unknown. If anyone fell by the wayside, there were no contingency plans – the rest of us would just carry on.

The tour started well. Once away from Germany's manic holiday traffic, we passed into Poland with only a cursory inspection by the border guards. Slender pine trees lined the single-carriageway E30, the filling stations were plentiful and they all accepted Visa. At our hotel in Torun, the management seemed quite honoured to have 20 huge motorcycles slotted into their car park.

From Elk the road narrowed and deteriorated, though the border crossing into Lithuania was painless. From then on, tensions rose as the landscape changed from scenic lakeland to flat, bleak tundra, and we put our watches forward on to Russian time. Crossing into Latvia was tricky, and one of our group, Reuben, wasn't allowed across when a guard spotted that his Yamaha's number plate didn't match the V5. He was put under house arrest, and by the time a new plate had been TNT'd out from Britain he'd missed the tour – we picked him up on the way back.

As we rode further north and east the old Soviet influence grew stronger. Peasants emerged from grey farm buildings by the roadside, relics of the huge collective farms, each with an apparent standard issue cow and ancient blue tractor. Then into Estonia, where Tallin is the jewel of the Baltic states, though BMW Adventurer-mounted Mike never saw it. He was turned back at the border with a passport/visa discrepancy. The road had become like a supermoto course, alternating between smooth tarmac and loose gravel that threatened to rip our tyres to pieces.

Our biggest challenge came the following day, when the crossing into Russia made all previous borders seem like child's play. Formidable wire perimeter fences greeted us as the guards waved us into line. In groups of three or four, we were directed through no man's land to the first Russian barrier. A chisel-faced Russian in a faded green sentry box laboriously entered all our details into a computer before allowing us through to the next set of booths. It was basically the same procedure, three times, and the whole process took three hours.

But we all got through, met our Russian biker guides on the other side and rode the 90-odd miles to St Petersburg – we were only stopped twice by the police on the way! After a couple of days in that beautiful city we headed for home. As we rode back through the perimeter fence into Estonia, we were cheered by a group of Italian bikers waiting to enter Russia. We'd made it!

Entering Poland was simple compared to the border crossings further east

POLAND

Poland is a major east-west corridor for trucks, yet many of its main roads are still single carriageway. The motorway network is being extended, but old-style congested routes are still common. Drink-drive penalties are severe – if you're caught with over 50mg/100ml, this can include a prison sentence as well as a suspension of your driving licence. The actual limit is a low 20mg/100ml, so don't drink anything before riding.

The police can require tourists to pay on-the-spot fines in cash and motorcycles must use daytime lights outside urban areas. One downside of the liberalised economy is a thriving market in stolen cars and motorcycles, so take care where you leave your bike – a private guarded car park is best, preferably out of sight of the road. Most filling stations accept credit cards, but you should check with your issuer before leaving home that your particular brand of plastic is valid in Poland.

FACT FILE POLAND

Speed limits	Urban	Open road	Motorway
Motorcycle	60kph	90-110kph	130kph
Traffic regulations			
Minimum driving age	17yrs		
Drink-drive limit	20mg alcohol per 100ml blood		
Helmets	Compulsory		
Daytime lights	Compulsory outside built up areas		
Emergency telephone numbers			
Police	997		
Fire	998		
Ambulance	999		
Useful phrases			
Wstep wzbroniony	No entry		
Wyjście	Exit		

CROATIA

Don't be put off by the lingering association of Croatia's name with war-torn former Yugoslavia. Though it's still illegal to overtake military convoys, you're assured of a warm welcome in Croatia, which is working hard to rebuild its tourist trade. And there are plenty of reasons to come here, including a long stretch of beautiful coastline, with breathtaking mountain country as you ride inland. This also attracts plenty of tourists, and the coast in particular can become congested during the summer.

The roads are pretty well maintained, though some motorways, as well as bridges and tunnels, require a toll. Speed limits are lower if you've held a licence for less than two years, and the police can levy fines, though you should have eight days to pay at a bank or post office. They may keep hold of your passport until they see evidence of payment. The minimum age for motorcycle riders is 18, and pillions must be 12 or over.

Spares
You'll need to carry spare bulbs, and if your bike is dented or damaged as you enter the country this must be recorded and a certificate issued at the border. If not, you may have trouble taking the bike out of the country again – the police are wary of unreported accidents.

FACT FILE CROATIA

Speed limits	Urban	Open road	Motorway
Motorcycle	50kph	80-100kph	130kph
Traffic regulations			
Minimum driving age	18yrs		
Drink-drive limit	50mg alcohol per 100ml blood		
Helmets	Compulsory		
Daytime lights	Compulsory		
Emergency telephone numbers			
Police	92		
Fire	93		
Ambulance	94		
Useful phrases			
Osiguranje	Insurance		
Ulaz zabranjen	No entry		

CZECH REPUBLIC

For the British, the Czech Republic is best known for the beautiful city of Prague, or maybe cheap stag nights, while many motorcyclists have made the long ride east to the racing at Brno. But there's far more to this country – with its mountains, lakes, spa towns and castles – than just that.

It's already one of the more Westernised former Eastern Bloc nations, but there are still some curious leftovers from the previous era. Motorcyclists are forbidden to smoke while riding (always tricky at the best of times). There's zero tolerance on drink-driving, and if you get caught, expect an on-the-spot fine of 2,000 CZK if there has been no accident. If someone has been hurt, expect a much higher fine and/or imprisonment. Level crossings often have no barrier, so watch out for trains, and you must always give way to buses and trams. To use the motorways, you must purchase a vignette.

FACT FILE CZECH REPUBLIC

Speed limits	Urban	Open road	Motorway
Motorcycle	50kph	90kph	90kph
Traffic regulations			
Minimum driving age	17yrs		
Drink-drive limit	Zero alcohol per 100ml blood		
Helmets	Compulsory		
Daytime lights	Compulsory		
Emergency telephone numbers			
Police	158		
Fire	150		
Ambulance	155		
Useful phrases			
Jednosmerný provoz	One way		
Zákaz parkování	No parking		

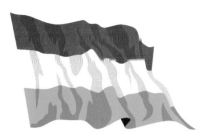

HUNGARY

If you like spas, you'll love Hungary, with over 100 thermal baths open to the public. It is famous too for its music, an international BMW rally in May and a Harley event in June. It also has a good network of mostly well-maintained roads, though you'll need to buy a vignette to use some of the motorways.

As in some other Eastern European countries, any obvious damage on the bike has to be recorded when you arrive, to avoid delays and explanations as you leave. If it gets damaged while you're there, you'll need a certificate from the police. And like the Czech Republic, there's zero tolerance of drink-driving, though you may only be fined if the concentration is less than 80mg/100ml. If you have to pay an on-the-spot fine, it will be in cash, which is also the preferred payment at filling stations – check with your credit card issuer before leaving home. Hungary is still a predominantly rural country, so watch out for unlit horse-drawn carts after dark.

FACT FILE HUNGARY

Speed limits	Urban	Open road	Motorway
Motorcycle	50kph	90-110kph	130kph
Traffic regulations			
Minimum driving age	18yrs		
Drink-drive limit	Zero alcohol per 100ml blood		
Helmets	Compulsory		
Daytime lights	Compulsory		
Emergency telephone numbers			
Police	107		
Fire	105		
Ambulance	104		
Useful phrases			
Egyirányú	One way		
Parkolás tiros	No parking		

BULGARIA

With its ski resorts and Black Sea coast, Bulgaria is beginning to attract many Western tourists, who fly there. But you'll get a better sense of how far to the east it is by riding. However, it's not a case of cruising straight in. At the border you'll be expected to pay a small 'sanitary tax', a vignette road tax and, if you don't have a green card, insurance as well. You may also have your wheels disinfected, but it's nothing personal.

There are new toll motorways (the toll comes on top of the general vignette) but many other roads are far from well serviced. Filling stations can be many miles apart in rural areas, where unlit horse-drawn carts aren't uncommon. Security is also an issue here, with instances of carjacking at night, the thieves posing as police. As icing on the cake, if your bike is stolen, you'll be liable for import duty on it though you can take out insurance against this at the border.

FACT FILE BULGARIA

Speed limits	Urban	Open road	Motorway
Motorcycle	50kph	90kph	120kph
Traffic regulations			
Minimum driving age	18yrs		
Drink-drive limit	50mg alcohol per 100ml blood		
Helmets	Compulsory		
Daytime lights	Compulsory		
Emergency telephone numbers			
Police	165/166		
Fire	160		
Ambulance	150		

ESTONIA

A small country (it's about the size of Holland) with a population of just 1.4 million, Estonia nevertheless has over 600 miles of modern motorways. This clearly underlines how the country has successfully embraced Westernisation – some say it has rapidly acquired a Scandinavian feel. Its northern latitude (the same as the top of Scotland) brings icy winters but long summers – April up to early September is the best time to visit. Summer speed limits are higher on some roads.

But there are still some reminders of Estonia's past. Drink-driving is strictly forbidden, and breath tests are frequent – speeding is strictly controlled as well. And while the country has over 30,000 miles of roads in total, less than a quarter of these, mile for mile, are tarmacked, so it could be the right destination if you fancy some riding on quiet gravel tracks.

FACT FILE ESTONIA

Speed limits	Urban	Open road	Motorway
Car	50kph	90-110kph	120kph in the summer
Traffic regulations			
Minimum driving age	18yrs		
Drink-drive limit	20mg alcohol per 100ml blood		
Helmets	Compulsory		
Daytime lights	Compulsory		
Emergency telephone numbers			
Police	110		
Ambulance/fire	112		
Breakdown assistance	1888		

LATVIA

Plastic & Speed
Credit cards are accepted at most filling stations (though check with your issuer) and if you've held your licence for less than two years you're subject to a general speed limit of 70kph (43mph).

Latvia has good and bad news for motorcyclists. The bad news is that only one-third of its roads are tarmacked: the rest are gravel or dirt. On the other hand, it has the lowest level of car ownership in Europe, so traffic is very light.

This is a flat country of plains, lakes, forests and white sandy beaches. Many visitors head for Riga, which is fast gaining a reputation as one of the coolest, most cosmopolitan cities in Europe. Eight hundred years old and with some fine Art Nouveau architecture, it's certainly worth a visit, but you'll have to pay 5 lati an hour to take your bike into Riga Old Town.

Unlike many other eastern European countries, some drink-driving is permitted (50mg/100ml) but the penalties for exceeding the limit are severe, so it's just not worth the risk. Speeding is also closely monitored now, and there are on-the-spot fines.

FACT FILE LATVIA

Speed limits	Urban	Open road	Motorway
Motorcycle	50kph	90kph	90-100kph
Traffic regulations			
Minimum driving age	18yrs		
Drink-drive limit	50mg alcohol per 100ml blood		
Helmets	Compulsory		
Daytime lights	Compulsory		
Emergency telephone numbers			
Police	02 or 112		
Fire	01		
Ambulance	03 or 112		

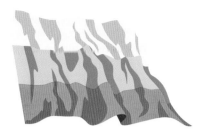

LITHUANIA

With over 2,800 lakes and dense forest, Lithuania is a scenic country, complemented by its capital Vilnius. It is also credited with starting the velvet revolution, being the first Baltic state to break away from the Soviet Union. Other attractions include the Courland spit and lagoon formed 5,000 years ago.

Nearly half of Lithuanian roads are tarmacked and the A1 and A2 class are up to Western standards, though potholes, mud and cows are common hazards on the others. Pedestrians in the road, and unlit horse-drawn carts, are common. You must be aged at least 18 to ride a motorcycle, and pillions have to be 12 or over. If you don't have a photocard driving licence, then you should keep photographic proof of identity (ie, your passport) with you at all times. The first weekend in May is a good time to visit Vilnius, when riders from all over the country parade through town. The police have radar guns, and treat drink-driving severely as well.

FACT FILE LITHUANIA

Speed limits	Urban	Open road	Motorway
Motorcycle	50kph	90-100kph	110-130kph
Traffic regulations			
Minimum driving age	18yrs		
Drink-drive limit	40mg alcohol per 100ml blood		
Helmets	Compulsory		
Daytime lights	Compulsory		
Emergency telephone numbers			
Police	02		
Fire	01		
Ambulance	03		

SLOVAKIA

Slovakia remains an overwhelmingly rural country, unlike the more industrial Czech Republic, to which it used to be joined at the hip. Tourists love the quirky capital of Bratislava, and the Tatra Mountains provide almost Alpine-like riding conditions. Add in castles, vineyards, spas and fortified medieval towns, and you have a country for which a two-week tour just isn't enough.

Most of the roads are tarmacked, though you'll need to purchase a vignette to use the motorways and some major highways. Motorways apart, the roads often follow old routes through towns and villages, with plenty of bends. There's a zero limit on alcohol, and, as in the Czech Republic, smoking while riding is strictly forbidden. Most filling stations accept credit cards, though it's worth checking the coverage of your particular plastic before you leave. You can ride a moped without a helmet in Slovakia.

FACT FILE SLOVAKIA

Speed limits	Urban	Open road	Motorway
Motorcycle	60kph	90kph	90kph
Traffic regulations			
Minimum driving age	17yrs		
Drink-drive limit	Zero alcohol per 100ml blood		
Helmets	Compulsory		
Daytime lights	Compulsory		
Emergency telephone numbers			
Police	158		
Fire	150		
Ambulance	155		
Useful phrases			
Zákaz parkovania	No parking		
Zákaz vjazdu	No entry		

SLOVENIA

Slovenia is tiny – smaller than Wales – but has a trump card in this part of Eastern Europe: it never got involved in the conflict that tore apart the former Yugoslavia and led to so much bloodshed. Rolling hills, dense forests and an Adriatic coastline give it a good start in the touring stakes, and the quality of its roads is underlined by the number of Italian, Austrian and German bikers who come here to ride. There's a big five-day bike show in Celje every March.

However, this popularity and the country's small size have a downside, in that traffic can be heavy in the summer. The motorway network is being extended (tolls are payable on all motorways), though this will probably attract yet more traffic. The drink-drive limit is 50mg/100ml, but you can still be fined below that if you're unable to ride safely. On-the-spot fines must be paid in local currency – refuse, and your passport could be confiscated. Pillions must be aged over 12.

FACT FILE SLOVENIA

Speed limits	Urban	Open road	Motorway
Motorcycle	50kph	100kph	130kph
Traffic regulations			
Minimum driving age	18yrs		
Drink-drive limit	50mg alcohol per 100ml blood		
Helmets	Compulsory		
Daytime lights	Compulsory		
Emergency telephone numbers			
Police	113		
Fire	112		
Ambulance	112		
Useful phrases			
Brezplacno	Free parking		
Placilno Parkirnine	Parking fee payable		

RIDING IN NORTH AMERICA

North America is a hugely diverse place – from the mountain roads of the Blue Ridge Parkway and the canyons of Arizona to the mayhem and lights of Las Vegas, it offers more changes of scene than almost any other continent. It's also huge, so distances can be vast. If you want to really explore the continent, you should be thinking in months rather than weeks.

The upside (outside cities) is miles of lightly trafficked roads and some superb scenery. The national parks are a must. They're all stunning, but if you only have time for one make it the Golden Eagle National Park.

Contrary to what you might think, it is possible to travel cheaply by bike. Fuel is cheap, there is free camping (if you seek it out), and as for food, the huge portions are big enough for two. The most expensive element of any trip to North America is likely to be the bike, whether you are shipping your own machine out there or hiring one.

Touring North America provides the chance to see a few of those iconic images for real

The USA isn't all motels and multi-lane freeways, as Louise Hillier and Gary Prisk discovered

Biker's tale – US
Louise Hillier

Although I had ridden bikes for years this was to be my first big trip. We packed our two Honda Dominators into a crate, flew to New York and caught up with the bikes in North Carolina. I had made the fundamental mistake of taking too much and over-packing, so my bike looked like a camel and rode like a donkey. After our first twisty mountain descent I just burst into tears. The bike was a real handful and the roads too difficult – why was I doing this?

But day by day my confidence grew, and I actually found myself enjoying not just the scenery, but the bendy switchback roads as well. There were so many great experiences, but one in particular sticks in my mind.

We'd been on the road for three months and were heading towards Montana. As the scenery had changed from mountains to empty plains I felt like I was in a scene from the movie Thelma and Louise. The road seemed to go on for ever and there were no trees, no houses, just a lot of nodding donkeys pumping oil. The only sounds were my Honda's single cylinder, and the wind.

The day hadn't started well – I'd been ill that morning, still had a stomach ache, and felt a bit sorry for myself. (Amazing what hormones can do.) In the distance I could see clouds, not fluffy little white ones but big angry black ones. Either they were coming towards us or we were going towards them, but either way there was nowhere to hide. As the first few rain drops hit my visor, it didn't seem too bad, but then it really started tipping down. It was like being put in a washing machine with extra spin as the skies emptied thousands of gallons of water over us.

Then the lightning started. Now this was really scary. Here we were, two little upright dots on a wide open plain as countless mega-volts of power sought to find the quickest way to earth. Each second I expected one of them to choose my helmet, or Gary's, as a convenient target. I remember looking to my left and seeing a bolt of bright pink lightning hit the field next to me. With nowhere to shelter, we had no choice but to carry on, but that didn't stop me turning white with fear.

Then as suddenly as the storm started, it was over. It must have been only minutes later that we popped out the other side. The sun came out, stronger than ever, and within half an hour we had been blown dry. The view to the far horizon was crystal clear, rain-cleansed in a way that only a good storm can bring. Meanwhile, the nodding donkeys kept on agreeing with the sky, and my stomach ache had been thoroughly scared away.

Travelling by motorcycle is amazing – you're in touch with yourself and at one with the scenery, and I feel privileged to have ridden through canyons, deserts and plains, and to have met so many people who made us so welcome.

You meet all sorts when crossing the US by bike. Louise and Gary carried on south, through Mexico to Central America

UNITED STATES

The US – land of the multi-lane freeway – also offers a huge variety of roads and wild country toe explore

The United States is the most car-dependent country on Earth, and yet there's a strong motorcycling tradition here too, thanks largely to the whole lifestyle that surrounds Harley-Davidson. Seventy per cent of US citizens don't own a passport, never feeling the need to leave their own country, and many of them tour it by motorcycle, so you won't be a rarity, at least in the summer. And if giant bike events are your thing, then the States has plenty of them, from Daytona Speed Week (Florida) in March to the Sturgis Rally (Dakota) in August.

On the road
To anyone used to the frenetic traffic conditions in European cities, American drivers will seem laid-back in the extreme. A long tradition of power steering, automatic transmission and big cars powered by huge, lazy V8 engines has made the average US motorist more of a cruiser and less of an opportunist. The downside of this is that they won't expect other vehicles (including bikes) to be travelling fast or to make sudden manoeuvres.

American freeways need particular care; overtaking is permitted on both sides (nothing new to users of the M25) and drivers often change lane without

RIDING IN NORTH **AMERICA**

indicating. When they do indicate, the rear indicator is a flashing brake light. Don't expect freeway traffic to be much slower than that in Europe either, as the 'double-nickel' 55mph limit has long since been abandoned by most states in favour of a 65 or 70mph limit.

Traffic rules vary between states – some will insist that you wear a helmet and keep your headlight on at all times, others won't. The helmet law in particular can depend on factors like age, experience, whether your bike has a windshield (a screen), and even your level of medical insurance. Daytime headlights are compulsory in some states but some (such as California and Indiana) make an exception for older bikes whose electrics might not keep up. The moral is to check each state law beforehand.

Most states also allow right turns at red lights, as long as you stop first to check it's OK to carry on. Filtering past stationary traffic is outlawed, and never overtake a school bus that is stopped with its lights flashing.

Direction signs aren't what we're used to either, as they often just give the road number and a compass heading (North, South, East or West), in which case you'll need to know the relevant number and direction as well as your destination.

Give way

Pedestrians crossing

Speed limit for freeway exit ramp

Railroad crossing

Interstate highway marker

US road signs often give the road number and direction only, though this one has destinations as well

UNITED STATES

Riding into a Western sunset looks idyllic, but watch out for lane changers who don't signal

Drink-driving

The drink-drive limit in most US states is less strict than in many countries, being the same 80mg alcohol per 100ml of blood as in the UK. Nevertheless, exceeding the limit is a very serious offence, and riders under 21 are not permitted to drink any alcohol at all before climbing onto a bike.

Filling up

America deals in gallons, not litres, but these are (surprisingly) smaller than the imperial gallon at 3.8 litres. So always fill your tank, as otherwise you'll be buying less go-juice than you might think. Although America is a motorised society, filling stations can still be far apart in the more remote areas, so keep your bike's range and fuel level in mind. Many gas stations will require you to pay up before you starting filling.

FACT FILE UNITED STATES

Speed limits	Urban	Open road	Motorway
Motorcycle	30mph	65mph	70mph
Traffic regulations			
Minimum driving age	16yrs		
Drink-drive limit	80mg alcohol per 100ml blood (zero for under 21yrs)		
Helmets	Varies according to state		
Daytime lights	Varies according to state		
Emergency telephone numbers			
Police	911		
Fire	911		
Ambulance	911		

In downtown New York, you'll be outnumbered by the yellow taxis, and on the open road, by Harleys

CANADA

Serious hazard – detour if necessary

No overtaking

Unsurfaced road ahead

School zone: speed limit applies 8am to 5pm on school days

30 km/h

Playground zone: speed limit applies dawn to dusk every day

30 km/h

As a biking country, Canada is quite similar to the US – the wide open spaces, lack of congestion and generally laid back drivers, plus, of course, scenery that is stunning in its beauty and variety. But fuel isn't quite so cheap (though still a bargain by European standards) and there are fewer differences between the laws of different states. The exception is Quebec, which retains a strong link with its French heritage. Across Canada, distances are measured in kilometres, not miles.

On the road
As in the US, right turns are allowed against red lights (Quebec being the honourable exception), as long as the way is clear. At multiple junctions, whoever gets there first has right of way, but pedestrians will always have right of way at all junctions without traffic lights. As in the US, there's a similar no-overtaking rule for stationary school buses with flashing red lights, but flashing amber means you can overtake with caution. A speed limit of 30kph (18mph) may apply in school zones during school hours.

Wildlife
Wild animals are a particular hazard in many parts of Canada, simply because of the more sparse population and lower traffic levels. Moose and bear are large, solid creatures, and if you hit one you're likely to come off worst. In wilder areas and on minor roads, it may be some time before another vehicle comes past. So take great care in forested country, where animals can appear on the road without warning, and try to avoid riding at night.

FACT FILE CANADA*

Speed limits	Urban	Open road	Motorway
Motorcycle	50kph	80kph	100kph
Traffic regulations			
Minimum driving age	16yrs		
Drink-drive limit	50mg alcohol per 100ml blood		
Helmets	Compulsory		
Daytime lights	Compulsory		
Emergency telephone numbers			
Police	911		
Fire	911		
Ambulance	911		
Applies to British Columbia. Regulations may differ in other provinces			

Hit one of Canada's large wild animals and you are likely to come off worst

RIDING IN
AUSTRALASIA

If you're seeking stunning scenery and want mile after mile of wide open spaces that are easy to get to, then head for the Antipodes. Australia and New Zealand offer an amazing diversity of touring conditions within a relatively small area. As a bonus, they drive on the left and the locals speak English (after a fashion).

But touring the Outback isn't a two-wheeled stroll in the park. You can make the trip as challenging as you like, as Oz and New Zealand offer tooth-grindingly hard off-road trails and roller-coaster pot-holed tarmac as well as the smooth sort. Wherever you ride, you need to be on the lookout for wildlife – kangaroos in Australia, sheep in New Zealand – though local drivers are generally pretty laid-back, with the exception of those monster road trains.

If Australia's mega-distances seem a bit daunting, then do consider New Zealand, where everything is closer together and there's nearly always something new around the next bend.

They speak English, drive on the left and have beautiful countries, both in New Zealand and Australia

Road trains deserve respect!

Biker's tale – Australia
Sam Manicom

The open roads of Australia can give you the sensation of flying on two wheels. But that surreal feeling is countered by our lack of experience of riding such long roads in fierce heat. In the Outback you can spend days riding through unchanged terrain; it can be completely flat, with soil the same colour as the road lined with vegetation of identical height and type. And the road can be so straight that it disappears as the proverbial dot on the horizon. This can make for fantastic thinking time, but it can also be mind numbing, which with the heat of the Outback makes for a dangerous combination.

I'd planned a 600-mile ride one day, which I thought would make for a long trip, but was do-able. In the event, it nearly killed me.

I used commonsense and tried to get it right, setting off at 6.30am. I like that time of the day in Oz, as the low light gives you the best views of the Outback. The colours are more vivid and less warped by heat haze than they are later in the day. But the real issue is that the cool is safer and a far more comfortable time to ride. A sore backside just isn't the worry in comparison to the real danger.

Anyway, apart from stops to guzzle water, I just pointed the bike down the arrow-straight asphalt for hour after hour. Nothing changed, and the road was in such perfect condition there weren't even any potholes for me to play space invaders with. As the sun grew higher, so did the temperature. I was riding with an open face helmet and the asphalt blasted stored heat back up at me. My face felt as if it was being turned into beef jerky and I could feel my body fluids being sucked away in the slipstream. Despite drinking all that water, I was dehydrating, and starting to get very tired.

In that situation, the sensible thing would have been to stop and find some shade for a rest. But shade is hard to come by in the Outback, as often

RIDING IN **AUSTRALASIA**

the only vegetation is scrubby bush. But almost fatally, I made the fuzzy-headed mistake of not stopping for a longer rest-break, with the result that I fell asleep on the bike.

One minute I knew what I was doing and the next I was absolutely unaware of anything. I've no idea what woke me, but it was to a view of pure scrubby bush hurtling towards me. It was an odd sensation for those few seconds because I felt as if I was sitting still and the rest of the world was moving – fast! Then I really woke up into one of those proverbial wide-eyed moments and yanked the handlebars hard left. I just managed to stay on the asphalt. A second of snooze longer and a circle of birds of prey might have been the only clue as to where I'd ended up.

There are tales like this aplenty in the Outback, and the moral is simple. Although Australia's smooth straight roads look like an easy way to cover distance, they still need to be respected.

Uluru – Ayers Rock – is just one of the natural wonders of Australia

AUSTRALIA

Beware nodding off on Australia's long, straight, hot highways – it's easily done...

The vast open spaces of Australia's Outback will deliver a motorcycling experience quite unlike anything you'll get in Europe. But the long distances need careful planning – filling stations are far apart and you'll need to take regular breaks to guard against fatigue. Fortunately, there are good value motels across the country, not to mention hostels and campsites, but it's as well to bear in mind that there may be no habitation between them.

Ship or hire?

You really have three options: ship your own bike to Australia, buy a bike once you're there, or hire one. Shipping your own wheels is really only worthwhile if you're planning to spend more than three months Down Under. To a lesser extent, the same is true of buying a bike just for your trip, then selling it before you leave. But for stays of less than a month, hiring is probably the best option. There are plenty of good quality bikes for hire, both road models and trail bikes, fully insured.

Driving conditions

Outside its major cities, Australia has sparse population, little traffic and no motorways. So even major routes are generally two-lane, though well maintained, and with overtaking lanes on hills to get you past slow-moving trucks.

Outback tracks

Drive off-tarmac, and the Outback has a whole network of gravel roads and tracks, most of which are well maintained. They're tempting, but think carefully before tackling these. Fuel stops are even further apart than on the main roads, and hire bike insurance may not cover tracks, even for an off-road bike. If you do go there, make sure someone knows your route and destination so that they can notify the police if you don't let them know you've arrived safely. And however well maintained the track is, it could still be washed out by heavy rain. Whatever the road, take plenty of water – five litres should keep you hydrated on an ordinary summer's day.

Speed limits

Australia's Northern Territory is one of the few places in the world with no overall speed limit, but don't let that fool you into thinking that Oz is a speed-biker's dream. The police do not tolerate speeding, using radar to enforce the limits, and even in the Northern Territory you'll be expected to ride with the conditions in mind. In built-up areas the limit is 60kph (38mph), but it can be as low as 10kph (6mph) in some places.

Beware of kangaroos

Roundabout ahead

Beware – slow-moving vehicles entering

Stop sign ahead

Reserved for cars with three or more occupants at times shown

Unlike road trains or utes, motorcycles don't have roo bars – it's inadvisable to ride through the Outback at night

AUSTRALIA

They may look placid, but kangaroos can kill if you hit one – do not ride the Outback at night

Animals

Perhaps the biggest danger for any motorcyclist in Australian open country is the presence of large animals wandering (or hopping) across the road. Hitting cattle or a kangaroo is serious in a car (even one fitted with roo bars) but almost certainly fatal on a bike. Do not ride at night, and take extra care at dawn and dusk, when animals are on the move.

Traffic priorities

It may not be in the rulebooks, but it's sensible to give way to road trains. These 50-metre monster trucks can cruise at over 70mph, so keep an eye on your mirrors. The suction as they pass is a particular danger for bikes. On single-track country roads, pull over to let oncoming traffic past, but watch out for gravel on the verge. Traffic coming from the right has priority, whether in town or country, so be prepared for that too.

Fuel

The golden rule in open country is to fill up wherever you can. Know your bike's tank range (remembering to allow for higher speeds) and if in any doubt carry a spare can of fuel – heavy and awkward to carry, but it could save your life. Remote filling stations may close at weekends, so phone ahead to check.

World of biking
Australia is one big country, but its states can have different regulations, so crossing the state borders needs thinking about. I got caught out once by a border fruit check. They wouldn't let me bring it with me as luggage, and not wanting to throw it away I scoffed the lot – which gave me a really bad stomach!

FACT FILE AUSTRALIA

Speed limits	Urban	Open road	Motorway
Motorcycle	60kph	100kph	110kph
Traffic regulations			
Minimum driving age	17yrs		
Drink-drive limit	50mg alcohol per 100ml blood (20mg for drivers under 25yrs who have held a licence for less than three years)		
Helmets	Compulsory		
Daytime lights	Compulsory		
Emergency telephone numbers			
Police	000		
Fire	000		
Ambulance	000		

Australia isn't all scorched Outback, and the greener coastal cities make a pleasant contrast

NEW ZEALAND

Speed limit drops to 50kph in adverse conditions

Gravel road ahead

Give way to penguins

Single lane bridge ahead: you have priority

Railway crossing ahead

If you don't fancy Australia's never-ending Outback, then New Zealand is the perfect counterblast. The constantly changing scenery of mountains, valleys, lakes and coastline provide a superb backdrop to the quiet, twisty roads. With a fresh view around almost every corner, you can see a lot in New Zealand without covering mega mileage. The country is about the same size as Britain, but has a population of just 3.5 million, so the traffic is correspondingly light.

Road conditions

As in Australia, you ride on the left but sometimes have to give priority to the right. Another thing to watch for is that when turning left into a side road, you have to give way to any oncoming vehicle that wants to turn across in front of you. Nor can you turn left at a red traffic light, unless there's a green filter arrow showing. The glorious two-lane main roads, so quiet after congested Europe, might encourage you to crack on, but don't be tempted. The open speed limit is 100kph (62mph) and Kiwi police, like their Australian cousins, are zealous in their application of radar and speeding fines. Watch out for the signed Limited Speed Zones (LSZ) which drop the limit to 50kph (31mph) during bad weather. Some minor roads have a gravel surface, and bike hire insurance may not cover that. Finally, every school child knows that there are more sheep than people in New Zealand, and most of those are free to wander the country roads. Farmers sometimes herd them along roads too, something else to keep an eye open for.

Bike hire

It's easy to hire a bike in New Zealand, especially in the capital Christchurch, and for shorter stays this is probably the best option. One word of warning, though. Don't step off the plane from Europe and straight onto a bike – you need a day or so to acclimatise and overcome jet lag.

FACT FILE NEW ZEALAND

Speed limits	Urban	Open road	Motorway
Motorcycle	50kph	100kph	100kph
Traffic regulations			
Minimum driving age	16yrs		
Drink-drive limit	80mg alcohol per 100ml blood (30mg for drivers under 20yrs)		
Helmets	Compulsory		
Daytime lights	Compulsory		
Emergency telephone numbers			
Police	111		
Fire	111		
Ambulance	111		

Weather and accommodation

Weather is something New Zealand has plenty of, with a changeable climate to rival that of the UK. The South Island is generally thought of as more scenic than the North, but its west coast is very wet, with around four metres of rain annually – the Fiordland National Park has seven metres! The east coast is less spectacular but much drier and the north-west corner almost sub-tropical. Wherever you are, accommodation should be easy to find, especially out of season, with a good selection of campsites, B&Bs, hotels and motels.

Kiwi views can be breathtaking, but steer clear of the most rain sodden parts of the country

RIDING FURTHER AFIELD

Adventure touring is more popular than ever before, whether you class adventure as flying to Thailand and hiring a bike, or riding your own across Africa or through India. The well publicised round the world trip of actors Ewan McGregor and Charley Boorman in 2004 was just a high profile confirmation that motorcycle adventure travel has well and truly arrived.

205

In some ways, it's easier than it's ever been. The bikes are more capable and reliable than ever before, and one upside of globalisation means that credit cards are becoming a worldwide currency. Internet access is growing too, so you need never be out of touch with home. And because more people are making epic trips these days, there's a huge support network to help them: specialist websites, books and bike rallies. Other specialists will sell you a high capacity fuel tank or tough aluminium luggage, or even adapt your bike wholesale.

But no adventure tour should be undertaken lightly. For one thing, there are more trouble spots across the world than there were 20 or 30 years ago. The only way to be sure about where to avoid is to check the Foreign Office website (www.fco.gov.uk).

Road conditions can be scary, with far lower safety standards than we're used to in Europe, plus driving habits that appear to border on the suicidal. In India, the chances of having a fatal road crash are 13 times higher than in Britain – in Kenya, make that 40 times higher.

None of which should put you off. Most adventure travellers report that big trips can be vibrant, life-affirming affairs. And most come home surprised at the kindness and hospitality they encounter along the way. An adventure tour can change your life.

You don't have to fly, then crowd onto a train or tourist bus to reach stunning destinations like Macchu Pichu

Indian traffic has three rules, according to veteran traveller Sam Manicom: size, 'I was here first' and horn decibels

Biker's tale – Africa and Asia

Sam Manicom

After riding the length of Africa and through much of Asia, I came away with a valuable lesson in survival – respect. Take India, where motoring machismo sets three rules of the road: 'I'm bigger than you are so I have priority'; 'I was here first so I have priority'; and 'My horn is louder than yours so I go first'.

It's almost as if the Indian driver is out for your blood as he makes an instant U-turn right in front of you. (One friend got round the problem by fitting a massive truck horn to his bike – he blasted his way across India, having trucks pull over for him!) It's difficult to show respect for other people in situations like that, but breathing deep and making the effort can save you from potentially tricky situations.

Sometimes a simple handshake can make all the difference. I was pulled over at a roadblock in Kenya once. This was unusual because these hold-ups so often seemed to be 'irregular' revenue collecting points, and as a tourist I was normally waved through.

I was immediately on edge. A very smart but well-armed and sinister looking policeman kept me waiting just the right amount of time to make me nervous. Then he aggressively bombarded me with demands. In response, I climbed off the bike and reached out to shake his hand. The situation could have gone either way, but a firm handshake and friendly smile worked wonders. The sinister policeman smiled back, and a couple of minutes later I was giving a quick pillion ride on the bike.

Another example: on a remote road in the mountains of Ethiopia, just after the 20 year war had ended, I was suddenly confronted by heavily armed militia. It was a nerve-wracking moment. I knew that these guys were tired, probably living on the edge, and they were pointing their mini-arsenal right at me.

I slowly removed my helmet, eased my gloves off and holding out my hand said, 'Good morning,' in my best version of the local dialect. The first handshake was cautious but by the time we'd all shaken hands the tension had gone, gun barrels were lowered, and I was waved cheerfully on my way through some of the most beautiful scenery in the world.

Most people you meet on the road, be they officials or Joe Public himself, are often more nervous of us than we are of them. It makes them defensive, and that can turn a situation nasty. Showing calm, non-threatening, friendly respect almost always melts the tension away. Tempting as it is to stereotype the people we meet out on the road, they do just the same to us. But a handshake turns both of you into human beings.

In the West, many believe that respect is something that has to be earned. But out on the road, turn that on its head, and give respect until people show they don't deserve it. All based on a simple handshake.

Away from westernised countries, locating a simple fruit salad can be a challenge in itself

SOUTH AFRICA

You don't have to slog the length of the continent to ride a bike in South Africa. It's quite easy to hire either road bikes or traillies in Johannesburg or Cape Town, at a reasonable price. Or you can ship your own bike direct. The country has a reputation for crime, but this is mainly in the cities (where you shouldn't ride at night); out in the country, you should find friendly people and stunning scenery, but be wary of being flagged down in the bush, miles from anywhere.

Then there's the wildlife. Having your own transport enables you to spot lion and elephant in your own time. Big game is more likely to run away than put you in any danger, unless it feels threatened. Even so, if you feel safer watching big cats from inside a minibus, there are plenty of day trips on offer.

On the road
South Africa has a good network of well looked after tarmac roads, and away from the cities there's very little traffic. Most are two-lane, and it's etiquette to pull over to the side a little and let faster traffic overtake – many main roads have hard shoulders for just this reason. You still need to watch out for overcrowded trucks and minibuses, plus devil-may-care overtakers. One bonus for British bikers is that South Africans still drive on the left.

If you want to venture away from the main roads you'll sooner or later find yourself riding on gravel, but these routes are often relatively smooth and well graded. It shouldn't be too difficult even with road tyres – just keep your speed down and brake gently.

Road rules
Any accident involving another vehicle has to be reported to the police within 24 hours. At crossroads with stop signs but no traffic lights, the first to arrive at the junction has priority. Filling stations don't always accept credit cards, and although there are tolls on some main roads, tunnels and bridges, an alternative route will usually be signposted.

FACT FILE SOUTH AFRICA

Speed limits	Urban	Open road	Motorway
Motorcycle	60kph	100kph	120kph
Traffic regulations			
Minimum driving age	18yrs		
Drink-drive limit	50mg alcohol per 100ml blood		
Helmets	Compulsory		
Daytime lights	Compulsory		
Emergency telephone numbers			
Police	10111		
Ambulance	10117		

Having your own transport in South Africa means watching the wildlife in your own time

AFRICA

Africa is a vast and varied continent, which really deserves a book of its own. Arabic North Africa is very different to Black Africa south of the Sahara, and beyond this division there are countless variations of climate, topography, roads, language and culture. Most travellers agree that you'll meet vibrant and friendly people in most areas.

It's possible to ride north to south, on tarmac almost the whole way, though the traditional 10,000-mile overlanders' route via the Sahara takes about two months. That's if all goes well. Africa is far more politically unstable than it used to be, and sudden coups can close borders overnight, making a previously accessible country completely impassable. The only answer is to keep your plans fluid, and accept that you may have to change your itinerary as you go along.

But there's no law that says you have to ride right across Africa to experience it. It's possible to ship a bike to the west coast as a staging post to explore western sub-Saharan Africa. Or you can ship to the east via Suez.

Sand, mud and scenery

Northern Africa is the most accessible for Europeans, as it's just a case of riding down to the southern tip of Spain and catching the ferry. This gives an immediate contrast between European and African culture, like that between the US and Mexico. Morocco and Tunisia both offer a relatively easy taste of Africa for the novice adventurer, and there are even organised tours from Britain. You can also minimise the ride there by taking the ferry to Santander.

Both Morocco and Tunisia are relatively stable and offer a network of tarmac roads, though if you do fancy a spot of piste (track) bashing though the dunes, there's plenty of that too. It's tempting to just head off into that wide open space, but even if you're intending to do a quick 30 minutes and come straight back, beware. You need to have the right

Animals on the road are an added hazard when riding in many Third World countries

Local taxi, Uganda. In much of northern and southern Africa, it's possible to ride a long way on tarmac roads

machine – a heavily-laden road bike with road tyres will quickly bog down in soft sand, and will take a lot of effort to extract. It's also very easy to lose your sense of direction once out of sight of the tarmac. A surprising number of adventurous bikers now cross the Sahara, but you need to be very well prepared, and preferably riding in a group.

Heading into central Africa, and especially the steamy Congo Basin, the main hazard shifts from sand to mud – this is one of the wettest regions in the world. The tracks become quagmires in the rainy season, and though some bikers have made it though, paying to have your bike hitch a ride by truck is often the best way.

Once south of Kenya, things get steadily easier as you ride south. There's tarmac all the way from here to Cape Town, and Botswana and Tanzania are very easy to cross. There's still spectacular scenery and wildlife reserves to enjoy, so starting at the Cape and heading north as far as Kenya could give an excellent regional tour, all of it on tarmac.

ASIA

On the Taftan to Quetta road in Pakistan, don't expect all road signs to be in English

Like Africa, the Asian continent covers a vast collection of differing terrain and roads, from inaccessible parts of Siberia and China to the tourist traps of southern India and Indonesia. A favourite trip for adventurous travellers is to ride overland to India, and then ship the bike to South-East Asia or Australia. It's possible to do all of that on tarmacked roads.

The overland to India route is actually easier than it once was, thanks to the gradual opening up of Iran. There are regular police checkpoints in the country, but these aren't usually a problem, the roads are almost entirely tarmac, with very little traffic, and petrol is very cheap indeed, though filling stations are few and far between. Accommodation and food are also cheap in Iran.

Crossing into Pakistan is relatively straightforward, though you have to remember to switch back to riding on the left. Once again, you can ride tarmac the whole way, and it's possible to cross the entire country in a day. However, if you're after more of a challenge, the famous Karakoram Highway runs from Islamabad to the Chinese border, climbing 4,000m in around 600 miles. It's one of the most spectacular roads in the world, carving its way through cliffs and mountains, and is even sealed. Continuing eastwards into China is fraught with bureaucratic difficulty, though one or two riders have managed it by arranging everything in advance.

India is a relatively easy country for the British to visit. You ride on the left, and English is widely spoken. However, Indian road manners are something else again, with a mix of machismo, nonchalance and fatalism making for a horrendous accident rate. The road between Bombay and Ahmedabad is said to be the most dangerous in the world. Add in uncertain surfaces (even when tarmacked) and you need to keep your wits about you at all times. Riding at night, when many road-users don't bother using lights, is an absolute no-no. One alternative over long distance is to put your bike on the train, which doesn't cost much more than the standard sleeper fare.

Shipping a bike out of (or into) India is a bureaucratic nightmare, but once you ride out of the dock gates, you're free. You can ship to Singapore en route for Australia, but that means missing out on mainland South-East Asia. Thailand is tourist orientated and has cheap fuel, though local drivers can be erratic. Chang Mai, the wooded, mountainous north-west of the country, gives good riding both on-road and off. Malaysia offers quiet beaches and cheap accommodation, and though the roads are good, they can quickly flood in wet weather. Traffic and border crossings are relatively stress-free as well. Singapore is more expensive by comparison, but a useful crossroads on the Asia/Australia route.

Siberia is another possible Asian destination, and a few well-planned group trips have come this way, sometimes flying bikes over to Alaska at the eastern end. However, these are the exceptional minority. Unless you're very determined and prepared to put in a great deal of forward planning, riding across Siberia is probably a trip too far.

213

Sometimes in the Arab world, road signs give an English translation as well

CENTRAL AND SOUTH AMERICA

Crossing from the USA into Mexico gives an almost instantaneous change of surroundings, from the richest country in the world into a quasi-Third World experience. If you're intent on making the 12,000-mile trek from Alaska to Tierra del Fuego (the Americas, head to toe) it's something you will inevitably experience. But you can make most of the trip on tarmac roads, and traversing South America isn't as challenging as crossing Africa or Siberia.

In fact, in Mexico you'll need to actively seek out the dirt tracks, if that's what you want to ride, though there are plenty of them, especially in the Baja Peninsula. South of Mexico are the seven small countries of Central America, and though you can stick to tarmac, there's no getting away from tricky border crossings and regular stops by the police for 'inspections'. The latter are really an opportunity for a small bribe, and part of life on the road, but requests for more than $20 (assuming you've done nothing wrong) should be questioned. Asking for an official receipt usually sees the figure come down.

The small Central American countries can each be crossed in a day or so, though that means missing out on a different experience to that you'll find in North or South. There's great variety between them as well. Honduras and Nicaragua seem to have the most bureaucratic border procedures, while Guatemala and Costa Rica are the most straightforward. There can be big differences in wealth too. Honduras and Nicaragua are poor countries, but neighbouring Costa Rica has been dubbed the Switzerland of Central America because of its relative affluence, though it's said to lack the vitality of its poorer neighbours.

Main roads through Central America are mostly in good condition, but surfaces soon deteriorate on the minor routes. The drivers here have a murderous reputation, and in part this is justified. You can hire bikes in Costa Rica (including Harleys) and take a guided off-road tour as well.

What you can't do is carry on riding through to

South America. The obstacle is the 70-mile wide Darien Gap, a near impassable collection of jungle, swamps and ravines. There's no road to speak of, and taking a bike through involves a lot of dragging, winching and hitching a ride on small boats – eight miles a day is thought to be a good average. Instead, most people take the more sensible option of freighting the bike from Panama to Colombia, either by ship or plane, the latter being more expensive but far quicker.

South America itself is a land of huge contrasts. It has the wettest jungles and the driest region on Earth. Countries are poor like Bolivia, or relatively affluent, expensive and European-influenced like Chile or Brazil. Driving styles vary wildly too, something which is especially obvious after crossing from Ecuador and Peru (everything you'd expect of Latin America) to law-abiding Chile.

Wherever you are, watch out for street crime in the cities and ports, and crossing the Andes can involve some severe weather, with roads closed by snow at certain times. The famous Pan-American Highway runs down the west side of the continent, all tarmac and favoured by long-distance trucks. A quieter, more interesting route, but certainly more challenging, is to cross the Amazon Basin, continue through Bolivia and then through Chile or Patagonia. High winds are notorious in Patagonia, enough to sweep you off the bike. But everyone who makes it says that reaching Ushuaia on Tierra del Fuego, the southernmost town in the world, is worth it.

Spectacular cities like Rio de Janeiro are one of South America's attractions, plus the fact that you can cross the continent on tarmac roads

INDEX

M

N

O

P

R

221

AUTHOR'S **ACKNOWLEDGEMENTS**

This book would never have been finished without the help of many people. So thanks are due to (in no particular order) Peter Avard, Louise Hillier, Birgit Schunemann, Sam Manicom and Phil Butler, plus all the other motorcycle travellers who have helped and advised me. Louise also drew the bikers' tips illustration. Thanks also to Haynes for taking the idea on board, and to my wife Anna for her endless patience.

PHOTOGRAPHIC CREDITS

Peter Avard (www.msltours.co.uk): 6, 8, 11, 16, 26, 29, 80, 81, 88, 154, 172, 173

Phil Butler (www.bike-astur.com): 62, 107, 155

Robert Davies: 48, 50, 55, 57

Peter Henshaw: 19, 21, 22, 23, 25, 27, 28, 30, 33, 45, 56, 57, 65, 66, 88, 89, 113, 116, 118, 119, 120, 122, 141

Louise Hillier/Gary Prisk: 44, 72, 96, 104, 186, 189, 193

Sam Manicom/Birgit Schunemann: 24, 31, 32, 59, 79, 87, 91, 92, 103, 105, 106, 114, 194, 198, 206

Laurence Turner: 12, 18, 108